BORN
PREGNANT

BORN
PREGNANT

DISCOVERING THE LIFE YOU WERE BORN TO LIVE

ERIC NICHOLS

TATE PUBLISHING
AND ENTERPRISES, LLC

Published by Tate Publishing & Enterprises, LLC
127 E. Trade Center Terrace | Mustang, Oklahoma 73064 USA
1.888.361.9473 | www.tatepublishing.com

Tate Publishing is committed to excellence in the publishing industry. The company reflects the philosophy established by the founders, based on Psalm 68:11,
"The Lord gave the word and great was the company of those who published it."

Book design copyright © 2016 by Tate Publishing, LLC. All rights reserved.
Cover design by Joshua Rafols
Interior design by Shieldon Alcasid

Published in the United States of America

ISBN: 978-1-68301-309-9
1. Religion / Christian Life / Personal Growth
2. Self-Help / Personal Growth / Success
16.04.25

This book is dedicated to my beautiful wife, Debbie, whose unwavering love and support has inspired me to do and to be all that God has called me to be.

To my children—Eric Jr., Sharaia, Asia, and Mark—for always making me feel like the S on my chest never faded even when you discovered I'm just human.

To my friend and mentor Dr. Vandy Colter, who taught me to dream and to reach.

To William Reed, whose love ignited a fire of creation in me.

To Monica Bailey-Washington, your confidence in me is unparalleled.

Lastly, to my mother, Louise Nichols-Young, your pride in me has encouraged me to take pride in myself.

Contents

Preface

APHIDS, ALSO KNOWN as plant lice, are natural, a phenomena because unlike any other creature, they are born pregnant. Or are they the only creatures born pregnant? Is it possible that humanity shares in this distinction?

Introduction

I DIDN'T ALWAYS regard the fact that feelings and emotions can be two totally different things. I always thought if I'm feeling it, it must be an emotion, but I've come to realize that not only can they be two different things, but also they can come from two separate places and serve two separate purposes. For instance, feeling proud: though it can arise from a temporary emotion, because you're having or regarding an emotional experience, it also can be a trait that is singular to a person, causing them to always feel proud. Prior to writing this book, I had always believed that emotions can't be trusted but have since learned "feelings" can actually be relied upon as sound counsel.

I do need to mention that the purpose of this book isn't to draw any distinctions between your emotions and your feelings. However, my hope and intent is this book will help you understand why you are feeling some of the things you have been feeling and how they are singular to you. This book was written to assist you in discovering the intelligence behind what you, and perhaps others, may have thought were silly feelings.

As we take this journey together, you will soon discover that this book was commissioned to help you connect with the you you've been feeling and how what you've been feeling all your life or just recently is actually the answer to a question you have been asking.

Lastly, the primary purpose of this book is to announce to you that you're pregnant and not only convince you of that but also get you to accept that you were born that way.

I'm sure that has engendered many questions already, from "Who does he think he is to make such an absurd statement?" to "Where did the insanity of such an unmitigated proposition arise from?" to "Have you considered my age, gender, and even more importantly, have you considered biology?" to "Saying I'm pregnant is one thing, but to say I was born this way is something totally different?"

I knew you would have many questions. In fact, I suspect you have far more than those I listed already, so let's start there; let's start with a question. Meet me in chapter 1 as we look at nine chapters and stages (much like the nine months of pregnancy) you will go through to give birth to the greatness in you.

1

You're Pregnant? The Question

AT SOME POINT—PERHAPS it was in the midst of frustration or in a moment of idle thought— whenever and for whatever reason, we all did it, we all asked the Question "There has to be more than this?" Am I right, does that sound familiar? I thought so. Great. Though my sanity is still in question, at least we're already on the same page.

Now here's the not-so-good news: although there aren't many questions that are more significant than this one, most of us rarely stick around for the answer to come. Perhaps it's because for some of us, we thought we were having a moment; no matter how familiar that moment may be to us, we convinced ourselves we were just us having a moment, and so we moved on to our routines.

Wait, pump your brakes! You were right; you were having a moment, a significant one! A life-changing one! A futuristic one—well, okay, perhaps not a futuristic one, but one that is most certainly connected to your future.

If what you are currently experiencing is somehow connected to your future, then it's important to at least ask yourself, "Am I pregnant?" Why ask yourself this? *Because only the question that is being asked will ever have an opportunity to be answered.* That's why we cannot move away from the question quickly or dismissively, especially since it's such an important question (which I will explain a little more in detail below). Besides, if we asked ourselves the question, we should at least demand an answer of ourselves. In moving so quickly away from the question, we give the answer permission not to reveal itself to us. And if the question has been asked more than once, that's because part of the wiring of the human spirit is to cause something to resurrect that needs and demands your attention. It's an indication that something is a matter of importance and the fact we haven't ascribed significance to what is outstanding.

The reason why asking if you are pregnant is such an important and significant question is because it isn't a product of your emotions, or just a revelation of your frustrations or discontent, but rather of something far more significant. It's an introduction or a diagnosis to something greater. It means you're pregnant with something—a gift, a vision, a purpose—that is organic to your existence. And your feelings of frustrations are often the vehicle that your purpose is trying to use to make itself known to you. Your reason for being here is awakened inside of you the moment you find out you're pregnant.

Reality Is Changed by Concept

I'm sure you're asking, "But why am I pregnant? And why does the question typically arise in a moment that I feel like I'm having my greatest frustration?" Because questions give way to thoughts and ideas, which is major for anyone who wants to move their life forward! Watch how this works: the initial change to any situation, relationship, life, or reality is what is first conceived about it. Simply put, nothing has ever happened without it first being dreamed, imagined, or conceived. *And every great dream realized has begun with a question.* So just imagine what would happen if you are asked a question and suddenly your mind is flooded by a stream of productive ideas. I'll tell you what will happen: your life will move in the direction of your thoughts and become the mirror image of them. *Life is not merely a sum of our accomplishments, failures, and experiences; it's a sum of our thoughts and ideas supported by our choices and decisions of what to do with them.* Ideas are the genesis of realities, so when the questions have begun, a pregnancy has already begun.

But why does the question oftentimes seem to come when you're frustrated? Because contentment is the enemy of progress and destiny. I believe it's fair to say that no one moves from beyond where they are when they are content to be where they are. That being the case, we need to understand that moments of frustration aren't simply to be used just for us to complain but to envision more and become more than what we are now. All complaining isn't negative or a sign of someone who's ungrateful, but sometimes, the one complaining is trying to teach someone else how to treat them.

The same thing holds true with your life and purpose; your complaint is simply the beginning of you creating and rearranging the conditions for greatness in your life. Your complaint means you have a greater vision for your life. Often, complaining provides much-needed clarity, and that's major, because *a lack of vision will cause you to arrive late for the moment you were destined for.*

Your Body Has Been Keeping Secrets From You

It amazes me how you can fully be living a reality you aren't yet aware exists and yet naturally make accommodations and allowances for that reality. For instance, it's amazing how the body is fully aware well before the woman knows that she is pregnant. Her body automatically begins to comply with her reality and makes accommodations for it; her cycle naturally ceases.

Your spirit (inner man) knows you have purpose well ahead of you. You start to experience symptoms that you probably likened to your emotions or frustrations when the truth is you're pregnant. When the normal begins to feel odd—or even old—your change, greater and tomorrow are calling. Even when you become bored, don't dismiss it, because boredom is creativity wasting an opportunity.

> Remember ye not the former things, neither consider the things of old. Behold, I will do a new thing; now it shall spring forth; shall ye not know it? I will even make a way in the wilderness, and rivers in the desert. (Isa. 43:18–19, KJV)

So when things feel odd, the "cycle" has ceased; the dreamer is pregnant with a dream, the visionary is pregnant with a new vision, the ordinary is pregnant with an extraordinary idea. Look for them, anticipate them; in doing so, you give permission for them to come. You give permission to yourself to be pregnant. And what you give permission to, you will create the environment for it, make allowances for it, and participate in it becoming a reality.

Don't do what many people have done; they flunk in their own life! Many people are great students of other things but poor students of their own life. Therefore, they are unable to detect their own pregnancy and misdiagnose it as their circumstance instead of their opportunity. It's very possible to go through extended periods of your life and not know you are pregnant or, even worse, to terminate what you never knew you were carrying! Your inner man reacts to a greater tomorrow that it knows still exists, the one you may have mentally buried. Frustrations are the doors that let dreams out; feelings are the radar for truth. It's how you discover there is more than this. So be great, be unique, be pregnant!

Say It: I'm Pregnant!

We all talk to ourselves; even when we aren't listening, we are hearing it. And perhaps we ought to actually start to listen to what we are saying, especially since the *conversation we're having with ourselves now is something we're unknowingly deciding about ourselves and about our future.*

Our internal conversations are where external realities are decided. The conditions of tomorrow are birthed either out of the conduct, choices, or conversations of today, if not all three. Many of us are currently having conversations with ourselves that are future related. We are already deciding if we want or deserve a reality or an opportunity that has yet to present itself to us.

Your inner conversations are your thoughts, and thoughts become your words and your actions, ultimately becoming reality. So you have to tell yourself you're pregnant with greatness, a great idea, or whatever it is you believe, and now realize you are pregnant with it. *You will never attempt in your life what you haven't accomplished in your mind.* Tell yourself, or you won't stay pregnant for long; your doubt will cause your mind to become a miscarrying womb.

Say it: "I'm pregnant." And now say what you're pregnant with. Why? Because you can only give birth to what you're pregnant with. The question we initially started out with proves how fertile your mind is. It has the ability to conceive a reality that you have never seen, touched, or even encountered. Yet it accepts the existence of it; so much so that the reality you are currently living begins to fail in comparison to the one you only subconsciously tapped into.

Are You Awake?

It is my hope that what I have shared with you has awakened you and will awaken something in you. If so, don't go back to sleep. Those who are awakened by a purpose, a dream, or a vision and decide to go back to sleep will awaken to a nightmare of missed opportunity and regret. And oftentimes, regret is looking back and seeing opportunity for the first time. Don't let that be you; since you are awake, stay awake. An awakening and change are two sides of the same coin; you can't change what you decide to remain asleep on. You can't change your life or the course of your future by going back to sleep now. Besides, this is no longer about you; you're pregnant now, there's something else very precious that is subjected to your choices. *Oh yeah, you might want to make a mental note of the fact that your life, dreams, visions, goals, and purpose are at the mercy of your choices.* So stay awake because there is something worth staying awake for. Remember, you are pregnant, and you were actually born this way. In fact, every person on this earth was: woman, man, girl, or boy. That's right—everyone!

How Did I Get Here? Better Yet, Who's the Daddy?

Okay, humor me just for a minute. Let's say you accepted this outrageous belief that you very well may be pregnant. And now the question I'm sure you're asking (especially men) is how and, "Who's the daddy?"

To answer how, it's best if I start with answering who. Brace yourself, I think it could be your neighbor; or it's possible that it's your coworker who sits across from you; potentially, it's someone you don't remember; even more so, there is a greater possibility it's someone you never even met! Who am I kidding, what you are pregnant with may have multiple fathers! What?

Since I have included the entire world's population in this premise, I think we should not only ask how but also why. Because the *why* is the answer to the *how* and the *who*. Every last one of us were born to do something, and that something is the answer to "Why am I here?" "How did I get pregnant," and "Who is the daddy?" That something is purpose; every last person that has and will walk the face of this earth arrived here pregnant with purpose. And it is that purpose that is both the cause and the explanation of your existence.

There's A Need

Necessity necessitates purpose. In other words, purpose is a divine response to a human need. What drives purpose is God's fulfillment of a promise, His answer to a prayer, or His response to a need. I don't know if you caught that or not, but that was your cue to get excited!

Why? Because I just confirmed what you have always believed; yes, you are God's answer; you are God's gift to the world!

> *Also I heard the voice of the Lord, saying, Whom shall I send, and who will go for us? Then said I, Here am I; send me. (Isa. 6:8, KJV)*

Every last one of us was placed here because there was a need for us. Purpose is your divine assignment that is connected to your human existence. However, you are not only supposed to have an existence but also a presence. Because every purpose in life is to either meet a human need or answer a human question. Purpose is simply finding something other than you to serve. Oh no, he didn't just call me God's gift to the world and then turn around and say I'm supposed to serve! God has never created a person or given a gift that was not supposed to serve someone else or something else.

> *Just as the Son of Man did not come to be served, but to serve, and to give his life as a ransom for many. (Matt. 20:28, NIV)*

To best serve them or your purpose, you have to go where you are needed. If we're honest with one another, this is contrary to human nature because everybody wants to go where they are wanted, but your greatest significance is manifested when you find out where you're needed.

I'm not opposed to people finding out their worth; in fact, for many reasons, I recommend it. But I think it's more important to find out your significance. *Yes, I agree you have something to bring to the table, but what good will it do you or those sitting at the table if what you're bringing is not needed there?* This is why many people are confused because they know their worth but can't figure out why so many people have rejected or walked out on them or let them go. The answer is that your true value isn't your worth, it's your significance. What you bring into a relationship, organization, or life itself, that's needed by someone else is your true value.

You were born to give birth to something that will change and improve the human condition; to touch, to impact, and to change something outside of you with something inside of you, to be the answer! You were born to be a giant, because real-life giants are never measured by their stature but by their impact.

You can only own, influence, dominate, or even change a moment, situation, or environment you're active in. And you can only do that effectively when you have increased your significance there. That is a critical belief for me because you will always be significant to a job, relationship, ministry, etc., where you have proven you are needed. Being where you are needed as opposed to being where you are wanted is without comparison. Being where you are needed is being in alignment with why you were born in the first place. Why is that important? Because when you are out of position, everything in your life will be out of place. Besides, being where you are wanted is normally temporary, but being where you are needed usually proves to be permanent or lasts far longer.

We will discuss this more in chapter 4 when we look at "Your Maternal Instincts Kick In," but for now, let's focus on the notion that a real impact happens when you live your life in such a way and with such a purpose that the world is glad you did! And live it with a sense of purpose that the world is glad you were pregnant and had the courage and the integrity it took to give birth. That's legacy if there ever was one! Because a true legacy can only be made by the deposits you make in life and not by the withdrawals. And that, my friends, is the answer to the Question "Is there more than this?" Yes, there is more than this, but it's not what you take out that gives it to you, it's what you put in.

2

Morning Sickness: The Rejection That Confirms Pregnancy

I'VE ALWAYS BELIEVED my brain was much smarter than my mind. My brain is always decisive, fully aware of its capabilities, and extremely organized. My brain doesn't require supervision and has the unique ability to multitask without becoming distracted by anything else. Unlike my mind which can't figure out what to eat for lunch. My mind oftentimes struggles creatively, causing my imagination to surrender to my reality. Which isn't good, by any means, because possibilities are birthed out of considerations; what becomes possible for you is what is considered by you. My mind is often too inconsistent for my liking; it can't seem to handle one task without easily becoming distracted by a more minimal task. In fact, now that I think about it, my body is probably smarter than my mind as well. Because my body seems to be aware of things much sooner than my mind is. My body will automatically attempt to fight off a cold before my mind even gets to decide to take medicine. It's the genius and superior intellect of the body that I alluded to in chapter 1 that allows it to be fully aware that it is pregnant well before the woman knows she is pregnant. It is because of the body's ability to discern what time it is that a woman's menstrual cycle ends and another's life cycles and behaviors begin.

Not Just What's Happening But Why

Morning sickness is a revelation that a woman's body is carrying something it wasn't carrying before. Everything the body is experiencing, though natural, results in a discomfort because, suddenly, the body is shifting into a new direction. Your life works in the same way. Your life knows you have been chosen for a purpose well before you do. And when this happens, you start experiencing a version of morning sickness that's related to purpose. Sudden uncomfortable experiences are typically an indication that your life is shifting in a different direction. Change, whether planned or unexpected, is typically uncomfortable because in order for there to be change, something must end in order for something else to begin.

Change is uncomfortable because throughout most of the process, two different realities are represented. While change is in the process of happening, the old and the new are present; both your yesterday and your tomorrow have their foot in your today. This is similar to midnight, the only moment in time that represents yesterday and tomorrow, and also the present. With this moment come two separate temptations: the desire to hold onto what was and the impulse to pursue what could be.

At some point, yesterday will kick you out of it. This is why, when it relates to your purpose, the moments of morning sickness can be extremely uncomfortable to deal with. Especially since they tend to manifest themselves as rejection. Rejection is never easy to process or absorb because everything about it suggests you're not good enough, you're not welcome here, you're not loved or even desired. But whenever destiny and purpose are causing your rejection, it's really a redirection.

Though it may not feel good, it's the winds of adversity that will blow us in the direction we need to go in and initially chose to avoid.

When your purpose is the cause of your rejection, your preference will become the sacrifice for your progress. You can't stand still and move at the same time; you can't stay in the places you prefer and make progress toward fulfilling your purpose or dreams. If the treatment you are receiving where you are has changed, it's an indication your assignment there has changed as well. You have to be rejected in one place in order to be released into another; it's not personal, it's purpose!

> *But Jesus, said unto them, A prophet is not without honour, but in his own country, and among his own kin, and in his own house. (Mk 6:4, KJV)*

Familiarity will veil greatness. When people are used to a person, they can't see the purpose or the potential they are carrying. God never leaves a gift in an environment that will potentially suffocate it or smother it. Familiarity is a threat to potential because it has preconceived opinions and perceptions of it. What we know about something or someone is what oftentimes hinders us from knowing everything else we need to know about them. I used to think that ignorance was the source of bias, but I now see that information can be just as guilty. Therefore, rejection happens in many cases in our lives because someone couldn't see who and what we really are.

I've learned that we will always reject the presence of something when we don't recognize the significance of it. I guess in a weird kind of way rejection can be a good thing, especially since God will not allow you or your gifts to remain in a place where someone can't see them. Oftentimes, rejection is a primary and immediate indicator that you are pregnant, especially when you can't determine the reason for the rejection.

All fruit, whether rotten or otherwise, have roots. And if you can't trace the roots and figure out why there's a sudden shift in the temperature and treatment where you are, it's because there's something in the environment that altered it. You're being rejected because you're pregnant, and now your life has detected it and is reacting to it.

> *No man, when he hath lighted a candle, putteth it in a secret place, neither under a bushel, but on a candlestick, that they which come in may see the light. (Lk 11:33, KJV)*

Nauseous

Being nauseous is a typical, if not normal, symptom of pregnancy. It happens as the body adjusts to the idea of being pregnant. I'm sure many women probably found themselves saying in moments of morning sickness, "If this is supposed to be a joyous occasion, why this discomfort?" Believe it or not, feeling nauseated is actually an indication of an internal clock because it typically only happens as a woman is in the early stages of pregnancy.

Whenever there is a purpose, there will be a clock, and it's normally temptation! Temptation is a revelation of a divine timetable. When temptation, issues, and struggles suddenly begin to happen, it's a divine clock going off, letting you know something divine is either happening or entering into your life.

> *Then was Jesus led up of the Spirit into the wilderness to be tempted of the devil. (Matt. 4:1, KJV)*

Here is where things become a little challenging to accept because they may destroy your perception of God or your perceptions of how He typically operates. But that's fine because God never wanted us to have a perception of Him but a revelation of Him. Also, whenever God is moving us into a new season of destiny or purpose, He forces us to accept a different version of Him than the one that we are used to.

But he saith unto them, It is I; be not afraid. (Jn 6:20, KJV*)*

Because you're born pregnant with purpose, oftentimes, your most difficult moment and your greatest moment are one and the same. In every divine purpose, there will be a moment when your advocate and your adversary will double-team you. Believe it or not, heaven is oftentimes either hanging around the hell you are experiencing or the cause of it. When this happens, it's called a wilderness experience: it's the moment when God takes you into the wilderness and hands you over to something very uncomfortable. Not to be in its possession but so it can do its part in making you great.

Every purpose has a journey through the wilderness because the one that goes into the wilderness is never the one that comes out. The you who will go through the temptation won't be the you who comes out of it; the wilderness kills off in you whatever is a threat to your purpose. And it will develop the chartcter, nature and discipline you will need to flourish and prosper in where you are going.

Morning Sickness Is Uncomfortable But Normal

There will always be a conflict between divinity and humanity because you will always be anointed and flawed at the same time. So God either arranges or allows certain experiences to happen that brings your human side in alignment with your divine purpose. It's called sanctification.

Can I be honest? The sanctification process doesn't feel very holy; in fact, it feels hellish! And that truth doesn't get much easier to accept because the expiration date of sanctification is the expiration of your life; it doesn't stop happening until you stop being. (But that's a subject to be discussed in another book.) In order to calm your nerves, I guess I need to share with you that sanctification isn't just something that's happening to you, it's something that's happening *for* you. Everyone typically thinks that what they do or are currently doing is exceptional even when it's mediocre. This is why sanctification is necessary; it comes to ensure your greatness and to break the curse of mediocrity.

But in order for you to become great and exceptional at anything, your greatness has to be birthed by the pressure you find yourself under. God will only release those into purpose and into greatness that He has already perfected in the wilderness. God doesn't waste your experiences, even those that seem as if they will never serve a purpose will end up serving in your purpose. When you are born pregnant, you will ultimately learn that you will not only be charged with giving birth to purpose but also be required to be birthed into purpose. And it's the moments of morning sickness that you discover that it's just as difficult as giving birth to greatness as it is being birthed into it.

I'm sure at this point you're probably thinking if this is what it takes, who would want to give birth to anything? And your feelings are not only justified, they are understandable. But as someone who has given birth and who has been birthed into purpose, I assure you there comes a moment when you begin to fall in love with what is inside of you. The idea of giving birth to life or a new reality connects with your innate ability to be a creator and a life giver. That's why some people will continue to show back up or return to the drawing board after a rough day, or even after failure. Because the life inside of them keeps giving life to them, their efforts, and commitment. The promise inside of them compels them to make a promise to themselves; the drive to be great vetoes the desire to quit!

I must caution you that being pregnant isn't just an expectation of life but also a process to life. So as excited as you are about giving birth, you must be just as accepting of the process to birth. People who are determined to fulfill their purpose in life can never afford to be goal oriented and adverse to process because process is the means to birthing anything worthwhile.

Whenever there is a process, there will always be a need for patience or faith, if not both. Giving birth is a privileged opportunity, so don't rush it, and don't become discouraged by the process it requires. Patience keeps anything from happening prematurely. And that's major, because arriving at your destination or moment too early can be just as detrimental as arriving too late.

Subjecting your purpose and dream to what it's not conditioned to contend with will put it at risk to the very situation it was supposed to flourish in.

While developing your patience, add your faith to it. Faith sustains the presence of what your heart is hoping for and what your hands have yet to embrace, be it your miracle, dream, or purpose. Also, keep in mind that the miraculous will always require a positive response to every opportunity that challenges your hope. That's what faith is; faith is your positive response to every challenge or adverse circumstance. Your response is always anchored in what you believe. Lastly, be encouraged that wherever you have to use your faith is where divinity already exists.

As you make the transition into your purpose, always keep in mind that every moment of morning sickness should be responded to with faith because faith is the distinct difference between sight and vision. Sight is limited to the here and now, but vision can move ahead and peek into your tomorrow. A faith that releases vision gives you the ability to see beyond what you're looking at. The today you're looking at won't bother you as much when you can see tomorrow standing behind it. A faith that releases a vision moves ahead of you to where you are going and creates the conditions for your arrival. It's a little easier to be patient when you know where you are going and when you can see where you are going. So add patience to your faith, because they are part of vision, and vison is reality in waiting. Vision is vital because it gives direction to both your life and your goals. And because whatever becomes a part of your vision will potentially become a part of your life, so what gains entrance into your vision will automatically have access to your life.

Don't Respond To Anything Temporary As If It's Permanent

Remember, it's morning sickness, not permanent sickness. Every season has an end, even seasons of struggle. Winter is always succeeded by spring, so remind yourself that you're on your way to a new life and new beginnings. Rub your belly, and love what chose you to give life to it. Besides, God only adds purpose to where He places His confidence. You are not only carrying your purpose, you are carrying God's complete confidence in you!

For many are called, but few are chosen. (Matt. 22:14, KJV)

Out of the seven billion people that populates the earth, you were the one whom God chose to do what He anointed, appointed, equipped, ordained, and chose you to do. Think about that for a second: *chosen!* There is no greater honor than knowing that out of all people throughout the history of humanity, you were the one preferred by God and are special enough in His eyes. It could only be my opinion, but that seems to be enough to want to endure some discomfort in exchange for the honor of producing something amazing.

Are you feeling more determined now? Are you willing to persist just a little more to carry your assignment to full term? What you are willing to carry determines how much God is able to accomplish through you and how much He is able to achieve in the places He sends you. What you are willing to carry ties directly to your full capacity. A tree normally has more branches than it does roots; the weight you are carrying doesn't even come close to the impact you are capable of having.

I admit being pregnant is a big life adjustment because now everything you feel and do is centered round what you are experiencing and what you will ultimately be birthing. But keep in mind, if God can't be allowed to make changes to your life, He can't be expected to change the world around you. There is never a great purpose without a great impact, but there is also never a great impact without a great sacrifice. The sacrifice of temporary discomfort is marginal when compared to a permanent imprint!

It's not enough to accept the process of morning sickness as normal, but you must understand that when you embrace it, you give God permission to move freely in your life. As much authority as God has over your life, He must have equal amount of influence in your life because God can't use anything He can't inconvenience. Too often we say, "Lord, I'll let you lead," but our actions say, "I'm not sure I'll follow." Accepting the morning sickness process, the inconvenience, is our way of saying, "I'm following. No matter if it's rejection, redirection, sudden change, or inconvenience, I'll follow because following your lead and plan will lead me to my dreams, purpose, and future."

Say it with me: "I'm pregnant, and this is normal!"

3

Strange Cravings: The Cycle

You will never enjoy or flourish in a season that you don't recognize exists. Therefore, how does anyone maximize what they don't recognize?

Seldom does destiny look like destiny, and seldom does it act like it. There are no neon signs, no public service announcements, nothing trending on social media, nothing broadcast across the airwaves, and yet it happens all around us and right before our eyes. Destiny will engage you long before you engage it; it will often make its presence known without having the courtesy to introduce itself. Yes, it happens, and it's happening repeatedly around you.

Have you ever had that feeling of déjà vu? Okay, that may be a little strange and weird, I admit. But have you ever noticed you keep having a similar experience or you keep having to answer a similar question? That's your baby, your purpose causing cravings. And the reason it's been happening repeatedly is because you were born pregnant but haven't been diagnosed until now. Purpose is often manifested through a normal abnormality or a regular irregularity. For instance, although what may be happening to you is a normal everyday experience, what's amazing about it is it only keeps happening to you! Other people are around when it happens, and they don't recognize that it's happening or that is has happened before. No one else is being asked the question you're being asked over and over, it's just you! Destiny and purpose are often arriving on the scene in a common repeated experience, one that's noticeable enough that you recognize that it happens frequently but not overwhelming enough that you could label it as something.

Pig Out

When the subjects or questions of destiny and purpose come up, I'm often asked, "How do you know what God's will is for your life?" Does this sound familiar to you? Have you ever found yourself asking this question before? Anyone who has a desire to be more than just an observer of life has approached or asked this question a time or two. My response is simple: "Pig out." In other words, whenever you want to know what God wants to do with your life, pay attention to what God is doing around you because God's will is manifested in what He repeats.

> *And the LORD called Samuel again the third time. And he arose and went to Eli, and said, Here am I; for thou didst call me. And Eli perceived that the LORD had called the child.*
>
> *Therefore Eli said unto Samuel, Go, lie down: and it shall be, if he call thee, that thou shalt say, Speak, LORD; for thy servant heareth. So Samuel went and lay down in his place.*
>
> *And the LORD came, and stood, and called as at other times, Samuel, Samuel. Then Samuel answered, Speak; for thy servant heareth.*

*And the L*ORD *said to Samuel, Behold, I will do a thing in Israel, at which both the ears of every one that heareth it shall tingle. (1 Sam. 1:8–11,* KJV*)*

When you realize you are pregnant with purpose, it should be natural to pig out. It should become normal to ingest as much information as possible that will provide you with a clear and precise understanding of what your purpose in life is. I'm of the firm belief information is the only form of gluttony that's not a sin, so pig out. Besides, you're eating for two now; you and your purpose need you to eat up!

Hungry Again?

Most things done repeatedly are not a mistake or a coincidence; there's either a choice or an arrangement. Whenever there is a purpose, destiny will be on repeat. Destiny is a sequence of events and circumstances arranged to bring you to the place you're needed the most. And oftentimes, they are a series of repeated events and circumstances. Oftentimes, when something negative happens, we ask, "Why is this always happening to me?" But when something positive happens, we relish in the moment, but we don't take note of the fact it keeps happening. Repeated experiences always have a similar cause, which suggests you are either being pushed or pulled into a direction or an assignment.

Whenever God repeats something in your life, it's either to draw your attention to a particular place in order to involve your gifts in a particular situation, or to perfect you for a particular assignment. Your repeated experiences are part of a process to develop you for what God impregnated in you. The process will always develop what's lacking in your character so that it will help you become proficient with the gift in you. But I don't want to talk too much about process right now; we will look at that a little later in the "Third Trimester." Destiny is manifested by a sequence of events and experiences. It has a rhythm that acts and feels like a disturbance to the normalcy of your life. So the repeated experiences you are having are an indication there is a change to your norm; you're being shifted, moved and positioned by destiny to the place where your purpose will take place. So pay attention, because what's pushing you is directly related to what's pulling you. Destiny pushes you while purpose pulls you. And they tap into your appetite for more; to be more than you already are and to do more than you have already done. It's that hunger pain, it's that question "There has to be more than this"!

Midnight Cravings

Being born pregnant means you are anointed to change something. And having repeated experiences is an indication you're mostly likely anointed to change something where you are, that' because assignment is always in your now, it's always in your present. The present is always the most critical period in anyone's life because in the present, you have the unique opportunity to change the effects of your past, shape the conditions of your future, and make history while changing the course of history. But the present is also the most inconvenient period in your life because most aspects of your life demand your attention now, in your present! And destiny and purpose are no different. Destiny and purpose seldom beckons you at a time of your liking or at a moment of your choosing. They are like midnight cravings: they awaken you, disturb you, and summon you in moments you are most comfortable with your current situation and in moments you're most uncomfortable with your current state. Purpose will often come knocking when you are sure about where you are and unsure about who you are. Midnight cravings!

A Taste For Something Different

If you're anything like me, you probably never get tired of your favorite dish. For me, that would be spaghetti. Don't get me wrong, I enjoy other foods like a nice, hot piece of chicken or a nice pan-seared salmon, but spaghetti is something I can never get tired of. I guess this means I'm like many people, I love certain routines and normalcy in my life. Because I'm a routine type of guy, I don't go much for surprises. I like knowing what's going to happen, and the thrill of the anticipation excites me more than something being sprung on me, even if it's something for my good or pleasure.

Surprises and change make me very uncomfortable; I like knowing how I'm supposed to respond to a situation, how to approach it, and what is expected of me. However, purpose doesn't like to comply; in fact, purpose has this absurd notion that you need to try something new. When destiny has arranged for purpose to connect to your life, it will introduce you to a stranger you know very well—it will introduce you to you!

Let me explain. Purpose is an assignment that oftentimes contradicts everything you have come to know about yourself. It is typically an assignment that is foreign to your background, your personal history, and even your education. The fact that God borrowed the Virgin Mary's womb and Joseph of Arimathaea's tomb reveals to us that God is not opposed to using rookies and virgins! Now do you see why I don't like surprises? The moment caused by purpose is different from the history of the person giving birth to it. The seed and the ground are different from each other, but a farmer or a gardener forces a marriage between them, and they produce something they couldn't produce alone.

When you're born pregnant, destiny forces a marriage between you and your purpose, and together, you produce something neither of you could have done without the other. The concept of purpose being foreign to the one charged with it isn't new. Adam wasn't born or created in the garden; he was placed there to tend it, which means he had a purpose that wasn't connected to his background but was directly related to his future.

> *And the Lord God took the man, and put him into the Garden of Eden to dress it and to keep it. (Gen. 2:15, KJV)*

As much as I dislike surprises, I had to learn to make allowances for some along the way if I ever expect to fulfill my purpose in life. Are you willing to do the same? Because the surprises I'm talking about are life adjustments, the kinds that make you uncomfortable and even produce feelings of inadequacy. Adjustments are oftentimes just as hard as change, but without them, nothing can grow, flourish, or be perfected for its purpose or become great at what it's doing. Much like a golfer making adjustments to their swing or a pitcher making adjustments to their pitches, it's fixing the mechanics that makes them great. The ability to make alterations to what you are already used to doing is often the difference between being amazing and being average.

A life story cannot be complete if it hasn't voluntarily been rewritten along the way, so accept that adjustments and changes are mandates of greatness. Besides, anything that doesn't change not only stops growing but also creates a culture of mediocrity for itself. The worst level of mediocrity is the level you reach after you have already reached greatness because you wouldn't grow. The danger of being conditioned by mediocrity is that eventually it will fool you into believing it's something extraordinary.

Purpose requires you to venture out of the places where you feel proficient and comfortable, and that takes courage. Who will leave easy and comfort to pursue something strange and uncomfortable? You, that's who, because you have already begun to show the signs of pursuing something much greater than your now! And because I believe you are starting to understand that you can't expect anything that participates in your comfort to also contribute to your growth. I'm of the firm belief that in order to stunt the growth of something, one just has to make it comfortable because whatever contributes to your comfort makes no contribution to your growth. Besides, nothing grows, becomes great, or proficient that isn't forced to strive.

This Isn't What I Thought It Would Taste Like

Rarely does anything new go as planned. And you will find that it's virtually impossible to plan for something you know nothing about or you don't know what to expect of it or from it. You're just hoping whatever this is you are doing, you don't mess up or fail. I won't try to sell you any magic beans here; that's exactly what's probably going to happen—well, not completely, just initially. Purpose often has failure at its beginning because failure is the most effective way to prove anyone's commitment and to see if you will show up for work tomorrow. It's not a permanent failure; it's training of your commitment.

For he supposed his brethren would have understood how that God by his hand would deliver them: but they understood not. (Acts 7:25, KJV)

Any new mother will tell you they have made many mistakes and even failed from time to time trying to raise their baby. With all the how-to books and parenting guides they most likely read, they still made mistakes. And what taught them the most about raising a baby, surprisingly, was the baby and their mistakes. Not exactly the teachers they would have chosen, especially given the enormity of their responsibilities, but those who have predetermined their teachers have ultimately limited what they will learn. Your purpose and the mistakes that you make in pursuing it will teach you what to do and what not to do in order to be successful at it.

If there are any benefits to failure, it's when it has taught you how to eliminate future mistakes. Failure and discomfort are almost promised in anything you do that's worthwhile, and they are certainly promised to be repeated when their lessons are wasted.

Mistakes are going to be made, and making mistakes will cause you to start comparing yourself, your gifts, and your progress to others. That's dangerous because comparing yourself, your gifts, and your progress to others will produce false positives. You will get indications that you're not accomplishing anything when you really are. Comparing yourself and your gift to someone else's gift will potentially create a sense of insecurity and failure. In addition, it's impossible to totally see your progress while monitoring someone else's. This is your baby whom God gave you to raise because He knew you were the perfect person for the job. He knew who you are and even that your feelings will cause you to disagree with your assignment, but more importantly, He knew what He could accomplish through you.

So pig out and embrace your strange cravings because you're going to need all the nourishment, experience, and information you can get to raise this amazing gift you have been entrusted with.

When you're born pregnant, you have to learn how to listen with your eyes. What you're constantly being exposed to is preaching to you and imparting vital information about you and your purpose.

4

Your Maternal Instincts Kick In

Why Are You So Angry?

The two most important days of your life is the day you were born and the day you find out why. (Mark Twain)

WHEN THE SECOND most important day of your life reveals itself to you, you get angry. Okay, maybe *angry* is a strong word. Maybe *disturbed, bothered, uncomfortable, turned* off. Or how about one we are already familiar with—*frustrated.*

Have you ever seen something that got under your skin and wondered why someone "else" hasn't done something about it? Or have you ever wondered why you are the only one bothered by it? I have a question for you: why hasn't it bothered anyone else the way it bothered you? It's all because you're the one assigned to it.

And it came to pass in those days, when Moses was grown, that he went out unto his brethren, and looked on their burdens: and he spied an Egyptian smiting an Hebrew, one of his brethren. (Exod. 2:11, KJV)

And Moses was learned in all the wisdom of the Egyptians, and was mighty in words and in deeds. And when he was full forty years old, it came into his heart to visit his brethren the children of Israel. (Acts 7:22–23, KJV*)*

For it is God which worketh in you both to will and to do of his good pleasure. (Phil. 2:13, KJV*)*

Your Maternal Instincts Kick In

It's you, it's your assignment, you were born pregnant with it, are you convinced yet?

"Eric, so what you're saying to me is my anger is for me to change things and not for things to change me?" Exactly!

Your anger is often a revelation that you are gifted to change something that is making you angry. Anger isn't just a response to what you disagree with; it's often an indication of a responsibility you have regarding what's making you angry. Indignation finds the heart of the hands it's been entrusted to. It's you!

The question why someone hasn't done anything is a self-directed question. Relevance begins with the questions you ask yourself. It doesn't matter anything to you until it has you talking about it to yourself. What's normally bothering you reveals your assignment, and your assignment reveals your gifts. Even those gifts you knew nothing about, those that have been hidden and only manifested as your emotions up to this point and not yet as your abilities. Yet you have been carrying them all along; you've been pregnant with them all this time.

And the LORD *said unto him, What is that in thine hand? And he said, A rod. And he said, Cast it on the ground. And he cast it on the ground, and it became a serpent; and Moses fled from before it. (Exod. 4:2–3,* KJV*)*

You'll Know If You're Needed When You Show Up

The strange yet amazing thing is that you probably had walked past what is suddenly bothering you on many of occasions before and nothing! But now, out of nowhere, your maternal instincts are kicking in. It doesn't seem to make sense, but when you're only out to do what makes sense, you will miss out on an opportunity to do something great. Besides, what summons you into action calls you into your greatness.

This is it; believe it or not, this is your explanation to your existence being provided by an experience and a feeling. This is you having more than just an existence, but it's the moment that purpose has decided it's time for you to have a presence. This is legacy reaching back into the present and grabbing hold of your idle hands and saying, "Let's get busy!" This is the extraordinary saying to the ordinary, "Move over, I got this!" This is your "I am God's gift to the world" declaration. So move, because those who refuse to act forfeit their rights to complain. Move, because nothing changes until something or someone moves.

The World Needs You to Do This; You Need You to Do This

Taking without giving will eventually leave you wanting. If you're always on the receiving end of life, you have only lived half of what life has to offer you. You will never know fully what life has to offer you until you add something to it. I'm of the firm belief the only way to extend your life is to give some of it away. We have to make deposits into other people; we have to meet a need in someone else's life. Now granted, that may seem like they are getting all the benefits, but let me ask you these two questions: What good is it to pass through this life if all you do is pass through? And what good is it to have been here and the majority of the world not only never noticed but also won't remember? I always believed that if they forget you it's their fault, but if they don't remember you, it's your fault.

Your maternal instincts aren't just kicking in so you can activate your purpose, though that's a good-enough reason as any for them start waking, but they are kicking in so you can finish narrating the story that your existence has begun telling.

When you're bothered by what you've seen or encountered, it's an indication you have also identified a cause with your name on it. That's major work on your behalf! You ought to applaud yourself because purpose is in self-discovery. You and your purpose are often in what you find out about yourself! When you find you, you will have also found your cause. Anyone without a cause hasn't found anything other than self to live for and nothing greater than themselves to serve.

You are here. No doubt about it, but what for? Just occupying space is to waste it; but to engage it is the only way to prove you're needed there. For instance God asked Moses, "What's in your hand"? He answered a road and then was instructed to cast it down and it became a serpent. My point is if you were born pregnant, then you didn't arrive empty-handed—you came equipped for an assignment and equipped for purpose. And wherever destiny draws you to is an indication that you already have what's needed there; it's an indication that you have a purpose for being there.

When God asked Moses, "What is in your hand?" , this taught us three important things about God's reasons for asking questions. I'm sure you're wondering, if God knows everything, why is He asking questions? Right, great point! God only asks questions to confront you with the answer, reveal you are the answer, or that the answer is in you. You are God's answer to a need humanity told God it has. You're God's gift to the world. And He didn't send you here empty-handed, you arrived pregnant and gifted. So understand that God never places anything in your possession that's not connected to something that's not already in your orbit (your surroundings). That's why assignment and potential are never far from each other; they just need you to connect them.

You must be willing to be used in order to reach your full capacity and leave your full legacy behind. Your imprint requires your fingerprints; you will only leave your mark where you placed your hands.

Your maternal instincts are kicking in, and to ignore them leaves humanity in the same condition you found it. Not only is that morally irresponsible, but also it's denying what is inherent to you and you alone. To ignore it is to say, "I know I'm pregnant, but I never want to meet the baby I'm carrying." To ignore your maternal instincts kicking is to decide to abandon what the world has so desperately been petitioning heaven for.

Why are you angry? Because the second most important day of your life has revealed itself to you and is requiring something from you. Your first most important day left you without a choice; your second most important day entrusted you with a choice. You are always free to choose what you want, but you may be forced to share the consequences of your choices with others, and that would be the rest of the world, both now and the future. Choose wisely, we all are depending on you. So on behalf of the rest of the world, I thank you in advance for what I'm sure you have decided to give birth to.

5

The Baby Shower: Your Circle, Your Supporting Cast

And they hated him yet the more for his dreams, and for his words.

—*Genesis 37:8 (KJV)*

It's only fair to believe that once you have good news to share, everyone around you would want to share in that moment with you. After all, who wouldn't want to rejoice with an expecting mother as she shares her good news with those close to her and anyone else who would listen as she excitedly reveals she has been chosen to bring forth life? So you would think.

But there's nothing like good news to reveal the negativity that's hidden around you or that's been lying dormant in your circle. When your good news creates a nonchalant response from those around you, it often reveals there's a shift in their heart to jealousy, envy, or negativity. It will serve as an indication of their perception of you and your dream because no one responds to you or treats you any differently than their perception of you. I know this isn't the news you want to hear, but you must accept that not everyone in a cheering crowd is applauding you. And if you're not careful, the sound of a mob can be mistaken for the sound of supporters. You don't want to wait to see pitchforks and torches to determine who is with you. Okay, it may not be that dramatic, but knowing who is with you as opposed to those who are not is essential to the success of any goal.

Can two walk together, except they be agreed? (Am 3:3, KJV)

The Baby Shower–Planning Stage

You will find that your dream will become somebody else's nightmare. Once people begin to hear your dream, they immediately begin to see if they have a role in it, and if so, they begin to audit their role in it. Oftentimes, when people can't find themselves in your dream or don't like the role they've been assigned in it, they will begin to plan for your dream to become stillborn. Now most people who fall into this category won't do it maliciously, but they will do it automatically because they are afraid that their presence in your life can't keep pace with your growth.

How people respond to your vison, purpose, or dream will often reveal the role they have determined to play in it. This is so amazing because this suddenly proves that your adversary doesn't have to be your enemy. An adversary can actually be someone who loves you but hates your dream. Anything that gets in the way of your progress is an adversary. I always believed that when someone has taken the time, whether it was intentional or not, to show you who they are, believe them. Why? Because it's never the rattlesnake's fault when it bites; it always gives you fair warning! A snake doesn't change its nature or behavior just because you decided to befriend it. So as difficult as it may be, always keep in mind just because something isn't currently hurtful doesn't mean it's not potentially harmful.

Wisdom and discernment mandates that you keep in mind that every voice speaking into your life isn't necessarily trying to speak life into it.

Your Guest List

Most baby showers are planned but come as a surprise for the expectant mother. Therefore, those who know her should have a sense of who should be there and who she would like to include on the guest list.

Your guest list is your circle and team. Whenever you're pursuing your vision, purpose, or dreams, someone will be left out, even those you initially wanted to include. That is an essential truth that you must embrace, regardless of how difficult that may be. Because whatever or whoever isn't supposed to go with you into the next dimension of your life will either become a drag on your progress or a pollutant in your next.

> *And Lot also, which went with Abram, had flocks, and herds, and tents.*
> *And the land was not able to bear them, that they might dwell together: for their substance was great, so that they could not dwell together. (Gen. 13:5–6, KJV)*

Why the change? Because the narrative never changes unless the principle in the story change. God doesn't rewrite your story with all the same characters still in it. Whenever there is a birthing, there will always be separation from the former in order to allow entry into the new. Some people must be severed in order for you to remain connected to your purpose. Some people are like scaffolding; they were only supposed to be there to get something up. And whenever scaffolding is left up after the building has been erected or the renovations are done, it becomes an eyesore. But take courage; anyone who is connected to your destiny or necessary to your future will never leave your life. This is one reason why I believe we shouldn't chase after people when they leave us, especially knowing whatever you chase after you give permission to run!

Now I must caution you: not everyone who isn't connected to your future or your dream will voluntarily detach themselves from you. Believe it or not, you may have a parasite in your circle, and a parasite will always hang on to whatever feeds it. And when we let people maintain a presence long past their shelf life, we become involved in a parasitism. A parasitism is the relationship between host and parasite; it is a connection that finds the host giving benefits and life to the very thing that is killing it. Whenever we expose ourselves to something that has outlived its shelf life, we suffer from it.

Have you ever noticed that you always feel worse after you talked with someone or have been in their presence? That's a possible symptom that you are mentally or emotionally intolerant to that person or are allergic to them. They are like a food allergy; they aren't poison, but *you* can't tolerate them. Like me and ice cream. I love it, but it doesn't love me back. So I have to limit my exposure to it. And that's a problem for many of us; it's not just that we lack the discipline to stay away from them, but when there's a history of loyalty or love for what has been proven not to be good for you, it will be difficult to separate from it. But you have to!

Granted, I believe you can't succeed at life and fail at people and relationships. In fact, I believe you have not lived to the full capacity of your life when you fail at people. Until you've connected with others or added to the life of others, you have shrunk the size of your own life. However, I also believe you should never have anyone as a part of your life who doesn't serve a role that doesn't produce a benefit for you. No matter who we are or who they are, we all must serve a purpose in someone else's life that produces a benefit, or we are causing a deficit in a particular area of their life.

That being said, I don't think significance should ever be given to anything or anyone who isn't necessary to the birthing of your purpose or who isn't essential to your individual progress. You should never have a person as part of your circle who doesn't serve afunction that assist with your growth and development. Your mind-set should always be you're here because you serve a purpose." Say it with me: *purpose equals presence.* Of course, the exception to this rule is family and genuine friends, but by the very nature of their title, they are already serving a purpose of some sort because love is the ultimate benefit anyone can produce in our lives.

Always keep this important fact in mind: when developing your guest list (circle and team), pace is affected by affiliation, so if you're experiencing a slowdown, it's possible you're being influenced by someone around you who isn't moving. You can't afford for anything that you believe is connected to your destiny or purpose to stand still while you're moving. Regardless of who you are, you will always keep pace with the company you keep. You will always run in the same lane as those whom you decide to run alongside of; what difference does it make if you come in first place in a race that you weren't supposed to be running? Who is on your list is just as important as the direction you're headed in and the destination you're trying to arrive at.

Gifts For A Boy Or Girl

What good is a gift that can't be used? When forming your circle and team, those invited to the table should not only know what to bring but also have the potential to bring what you don't already possess. Therefore, as you begin to pursue your purpose in life, your circle should include people who will operate as mentors, those who offer inspiration, a few who are allowed to have influence, and even some who provide intimidation.

Your mentor(s) should be more than someone you model yourself after; they should be those who take a genuine interest in you personally. No one can prove that they care about what you are carrying inside of you if they don't care about how you are doing. As a healthy mother will always increase the probability of a healthy baby, your mentor should want to make sure you are in a healthy place. They should also be willing to share their failures and mistakes with you and not just their successes. I always tell my children, "I made the mistakes for you already so you don't have to make them, and here are the lessons I learned from them." Granted, you will still make some, but you certainly will avoid some as well. However, the mistakes you do end up making will be those that teach you and those you are able to recover from. And those you avoid will be those that would have ended the dream at the mistake.

If I look up to you, you should have the ability to lift me up to you by the patterns you set for me and for the genuine care you have for me. That's what real mentors do. A mentor must be one who does more than help mold the purpose—they help mold the person.

Inspiration is fuel. Every new mother will have moments when she is not feeling very comfortable about herself. Her ankles will swell, her body will change, her coordination will be off. The last thing she will need to hear or be reminded of is how fat she looks. She will always want, if not need, to hear how radiant she looks, that she is absolutely glowing. In my opinion, this is most certainly true. When my wife was pregnant with each of our children, she was stunning. Don't get me wrong, she was always beautiful to me, but when she was expecting, there was something almost angelic about her appearance. Perhaps it was the love she had for each child that was manifesting itself in her appearance. Whatever the reason, I made it my business to always share my thoughts; mostly because they were true, but also, I knew as she changed, she would find encouragement from me telling her what I am witnessing.

I didn't mention this in the hopes of gaining some points with her when she reads this (although I hope I do). I mentioned it because I have come to realize that in most new endeavors, you will only be as good as your inspiration. You need people in your circle who will inspire you when your passion and confidence are eluding you. You need someone who can stir excitement in you. Dream chasing can be exhausting because it can develop routines that kill or threaten passion. Passion and creativity are two of the hardest things to repeat, especially when they don't readily produce what they promise. This is why you need people around you who, by their very presence, their expectations of you, or by their confidence in you motivate greatness when it's easy to be mediocre.

When someone has the skills to inspire you, they also have the ability to ignite a fire in you. Inspiration resonates with passion; it's a fuel that helps you increase the level of effort to do something that you wouldn't have given without it.

Special Guests And Reserve Seating:
Those With Influence

You need people on your team whom you've allowed to have influence—someone who has the freedom to be candid, not manipulative, but frank and persuasive. Let's be honest, making changes, going through changes, and giving birth can exhaust us. And it's typically the fatigue that is coming from your present efforts that will become the enemy of your future efforts. So receiving counsel from apprehensive people in moments when you're exhausted will extend the life span of your struggle and your unfulfillment. You need people around you who understand that doing nothing just because you're tired is the best way to cause a dream to become a casualty to inactivity. People who you give influence to must understand clearly the necessity of you having the right attitude in critical moments because you don't want to pass a bad attitude down to what you're hoping to give birth to.

Frustration is inevitable whenever your attitude and your desire are not related. So you need people around you who can speak the right thing at the right time to shift your attitude in alignment with your desires. If your attitude doesn't match what you are hoping to give birth to, your frustrations and your negativity will turn toward your dream. The wrong attitude will actually cause you to resent what you want.

An attitude shift is typically a revelation of a shift in your belief system. Oftentimes, a bad attitude isn't caused by a negative disposition but by the presence of fear and the absence of faith. Whether if it's a fear of failure, the fear of making a decision at a critical moment, or the overwhelming responsibilities that have now been thrust upon you, that kind of fear will always reside where faith has vacated. In the absence of faith, fear creates the results you dread, causing you to arrive at the destination you tried to dodge, and births the scenarios you want to avoid. This is why having someone with influence in your circle is important; they can not only sniff out your fear and frankly point it out to you but also, more importantly, help you face it.

Do you have someone in your life you can trust with influence? If so, put them in position. You will need them.

Those Who Intimidate The Average Out Of You

Anytime you allow people to have a critical role in your life who don't have like vision or standards, you position them to handle you instead of assisting you. That's why you need people in your circle whose level of excellence will intimidate any temptation you may have to be mediocre. Let's be honest, you don't need the assistance of anyone to be average; anyone can accomplish that all by themselves. Therefore, you should never have anyone in your circle or life who thinks you're average or allows you to be average. Those who intimidate you may criticize you in order to raise your game.

Criticize? Yes, criticize. Two truths you need to understand about destiny and purpose: everyone cheering you on isn't right, and everyone criticizing you isn't wrong. Next, your destiny and purpose are determined by critical moments, not critics. So handle the critical moments, and they will handle your critics.

Lastly, you need to understand that your circle is incomplete without someone you need and someone who needs you. So as you move into your purpose, it will attract and draw your audience, your support, and those who validate your significance.

As you form your circle, do your due diligence because no doubt there will be some unsettling moments ahead of you as you move closer to giving birth to your purpose.

6

The Baby Kicks

THERE'S NOTHING LIKE something real happening to confirm that something else is a reality.

At some point, the baby kicks, and it suddenly becomes real. Yes, all the changes you've gone through and experienced are indicators that you've been carrying life in you, but it's when the baby finally kicks that there is a level of intimacy that you have with it like no other. "My baby, I feel it!" What a wonderful thing for anyone ready to give birth to have the privilege of saying!

> *For, lo, as soon as the voice of thy salutation sounded in mine ears, the babe leaped in my womb for joy. (Lk 1:44, KJV)*

The beauty of being born pregnant is that we entered into this life with a Word from God spoken over our lives. A Word that sets events into motion, even those that will take place well into our future. When God speaks, there's an emergence of the reality that once only existed in the mind of God into the life of the one He spoke it over.

> *Then said the Lord unto me, Thou hast well seen: for I will hasten my word to perform it. (Jer. 1:12, KJV)*

The Word God spoke over you begins to move through reality, knitting one event to another. The advent of these events will cause His providence to seem like a coincidence until you realize this was all an arrangement and the baby is kicking! When you're living a life of purpose, there is a moment when you feel it, when you feel your connection to it and you feel it connecting to you. Though it doesn't yet speak, it suddenly has a voice, and it has your full, undivided attention.

As your purpose grows in you, like a new mother, you wonder, What is it doing? Is it okay? Is it getting what it needs? If it could talk, what would it tell you? And what does it want from you at this very moment? This is you falling in love with something you have not yet met, but somehow, you know it. Yes, this is you falling in love with it, you adoring the idea of it, and you loving the reality of it. Everything about it except its actual appearance is real right now—how could you not love it? There's no doubt, you're pregnant! And as terrifying as an ordeal that can be for you, the excitement is even greater!

An Ultrasound

Where there is movement, there is life. When you feel activity inside you that wasn't there before, it confirms the reality of your purpose. The reality of your purpose manifests itself as a new sense of urgency to bring forth what you know you can. But that isn't enough; you want more now, you want a visual of some sort. For every purpose or dream, there will be a vision, a snapshot of what is to come. Vision is God's will for your life that has now made its way into your understanding. Vision is the optical ability of your mind's eye; your mind has the ability to see things that has yet to materialize before your eyes. It gives you something to look at until there is actually something to see. Vision is an impending reality; it sits in the mind of the visionary until it enters into their life.

I have always believed that a reality that only currently exists in your mind is no less of a reality that appears before your eyes. When your baby kicks, it's giving you an opportunity to look inside of you and see it. Enthusiasm, urgency, focus, and renewed passion is your baby kicking. When you have these moments, you see what's inside fitting in with what's around you. When your baby starts to kick, it starts to rearrange the furniture in your mind; you start to see yourself living with purpose in the various areas of your life.

What Does It Want From You?

Purpose wants your attention! And you must give it your undivided attention because whatever holds your attention or becomes your focus potentially determines your next move. Purpose beckons you and sends for you. How exciting is that? Because what summons you can also send you, and what sends you is what makes you great. What can call you out of your past can also send you into your future, and what calls you out of being average can also send you into becoming great. So will you choose to listen and respond when it calls, or will you choose to ignore the baby kicking inside of you as if it's any everyday experience?

Why am I asking so many questions? Because I want you to understand that your choices and your responses are builders of your tomorrow. You can't separate results from the choices that preceded them. If you understand that, then you will appreciate that both mediocrity and greatness are choices. Your purpose is kicking, and your response is vital because how you respond to something will determine its significance in your life. How you respond to something will determine the role it plays, the function it serves and even the benefits it produces. So when your purpose is kicking acknowledge it, respond to it, I promise you will never regret the day you did.

When You Really Feel It Kicking

It's amazing how what was once a response is now a natural behavior. Without fail, just about every time the baby kicks, the mother automatically reaches for her stomach.

Nothing is driving you if it doesn't harvest your time and efforts and cause you to make adjustments. When purpose becomes a priority, you give it your attention and you don't wander aimlessly or recklessly through life because purpose provides direction and stability to your life. Whatever is a priority sets the beat that we move our lives to, because no one is ever out of step with their "true" priorities. When you're pregnant, so is your mind; you think like someone who's pregnant, which means you yield to the premise that you have to live your life according to the rules of your assignment.

The baby is kicking, and it's letting you know you have to live as if you're pregnant with a purpose. Your time spent, your efforts given, and your adjustments made all reveal that not only is the purpose you are carrying driving today, but also has brought tomorrow into focus.

It Keeps Kicking, And I Keep Being Awakened

It's amazing to me what constitutes as pressure. Something as small as a baby kicking can be considered pressure; it's the subtle reminder that you're pregnant and that truth can never be put to rest until its birthed. Being pregnant with purpose is a truth that makes rest difficult. When purpose grabs your attention, it also snatches your rest. When you want to go to sleep, the baby kicks and reawakens you. When you want to quit or slack off, the kicking of the baby ignites both passion and discipline, the two major qualities that keep moving you forward and keep you on pace. So if you keep getting up and doing what needs to be done, it reveals you're in step with purpose, you're in step with your true priority. What we truly feel about something is revealed in what we do for it, and what's important to us is revealed by what we permit to inconvenience us. I have always believed you don't really love something or it doesn't really matter to you unless it haunts your decision making.

The persistent kicking of the baby will cause your relentless pursuit of your purpose. When God called me to preach I was afraid to answer Him, I ran from my call for two years. I knew there was a call on my life, but I didn't want it or the responsibility of it. My acceptance of my call literally came from being awakened. For two straight years God woke me up from my sleep or prevented me from going to sleep altogether, until I said yes. And amazingly as soon I said yes I was able to sleep like a baby! The kicking of your purpose is the beginning of a negotiation, it wants something from you and you will want something from it. And the only way for the two of you to get what each of you want, "you" will have to say yes when you are awakened.

Your life is shaped by what's significant to you. Whether it's done intentionally or subconsciously, you will always cause everything that is controlled by you to come in alignment with what is important to you. Priority sets agendas, creates seasons, charts courses, encourages choices, forms and dissolves relationships, and engenders pursuits, therefore shaping your life. Whatever you're pregnant with will shape your life, even if you have yet to give birth to it. Purpose is now your priority, and everything in your life now forms around what is sitting at the head of the table.

Activity Creates Activity

There are few things that self-replicate. Change creates change, excellence produces excellence, and activity generates activity.

When your purpose becomes active in your life, circle, and environment, it should cause you to become active as well. And not just active, but your activity needs to mirror the demands of your purpose.

Your activity is where your potential resides. Let's look at it from this perspective; we commonly quote the passage of scripture in Proverbs 18:16 (kjv):,"A man's gift maketh room for him, and bringeth him before great men."

Although I believe wholeheartedly that your gift, environment, platform, destination, and audience are all related, I also believe that the gift must first be manifested in order to make room, and the only way to manifest a gift is to use it, become active with it.

When you have a purpose, you have a gift. Typically, your gift is something that comes easily for you but it will take others effort, education, training, and patience to develop. When you recognize your gift, use it. Your activity will eventually create the stage and the opportunity for your purpose to impact those who need it. You can't touch anything if you're not reaching, so reach and get moving! I don't necessarily believe you lose what you don't use, but I do believe you can kill its strength through inactivity to the point that it is of no use. Think of it as the wind: the more it stirs, the greater the force it produces. That's you, that is your gift, and that is how your purpose works.

The Real Strength Of The Baby's Influence Is In Its Kick

You don't stop being you, no matter how hard you try to be someone else. And you don't get to stop being pregnant just because you're tired or you're tired of the baby kicking.

When there's something inside so strong, nothing external can deter you, not even the temptation to quit. When you want to become great, give birth to your dreams, or fulfill your purpose, you must learn to ignore the conversation quitting wants to have with you. You must understand that you will never become successful at anything until you learn to resist every inclination to quit. You must learn to persevere. Perseverance is a lifeline; it keeps success and greatness from becoming casualties of struggle and the temptations to quit.

Anything worth doing, being, or having will come with noticeable struggle. But it's how one handles the moments of struggle that distinguishes those who will be great from those who will be average. Yes, you may have reasons to quit, but the will to be great kicks that notion out of your mind because to give up is to surrender who you are destined to be.

> *His lord said unto him, Well done, thou good and faithful servant: thou hast been faithful over a few things, I will make thee ruler over many things: enter thou into the joy of thy lord. (Matt. 25:21, 23, KJV)*

Purpose is your service to your fellow man, and there will be moments when you will have to serve and be obedient to your purpose when it's a struggle to do so. But the rewards are worth it because the favor of God follows your service and overtakes the servant. Your obedience is the only thing that you have that can add momentum to your destiny and greatness. So remain faithful, take the risk that obedience requires in the face of struggle, and you will be the cause of your own astonishment. I always believed that anyone who no longer surprises themselves has stopped taking risks and stopped trying something new. So try something new; instead of surrendering, keep going!

When amazing is within your reach, struggle will be within proximity. But always keep in mind dark moments are simply your opportunities to shine. The moment you're not feeling is your purpose reminding you that this is your opportunity to excel in your darkest hour. So shine because you will forever be defined by what you create, produce, and conquer.

Being Reminded That You're Remembered

Don't shrink in your moment when the moment is expanding in you. Moments change lives because moments change minds and people. This is your moment that will change your everything forever!

When the baby is kicking, when the intensity increases, it is greatness remembering you and reminding you to do something with it. Greatness always has a moment that will provide you with the chance to be remembered by the world. History, both divine and human, will only remember what you accomplished in the time and opportunity you had to do it in.

So the more you feel the internal pressure to be great, the more it confirms your purpose and dream's confidence in you. This is the moment that you must say to yourself, "If the baby trusts me, then I will have the same trust in my own ability to birth it." Give yourself permission to say I have what it takes to birth this, to give life to it, and to be great.

You will always remember what you decided to do when the baby started kicking, and you will always thank it for reminding you of the greatness you were capable of. And you will forever be proud of yourself for accepting its confidence as your truth.

7

The Third Trimester

THERE ARE LIMITATIONS to limitless potential.

I used to believe that being graceful is supposed to be a benefit of experience, but I found out quickly that's not always true.

Just because you have been doing something for a while or over an extended period of time doesn't mean you're able to do it gracefully. The third trimester of pregnancy is often one of those not-so-graceful periods. The expectant doesn't move the way they used to and in some situations aren't allowed to do what they used to do. There are moments in the third trimester in which you will feel that you're actually better at being pregnant than you are at doing what you used to do. Being pregnant has seemingly become natural, and what was normal seems like it's unnatural activity. Something as simple as sitting and rising often can't be accomplished without the assistance of others.

As purpose starts to reach maturity, you will discover more and more what was isn't. As you grow into your purpose, you will realize that there are things you will never be able to accomplish without help. Which isn't an easy adjustment to make in your thinking because up to this point, many of your natural gifts, talents, and even experiences have assisted you. But not here and not now!

I don't know about you, but that's hard for me. Not just because I take pride in my own ability to do things. But also because I've always believed experience is the gift your past gives to your future. Yet with all the experience you garnered from actually operating in your purpose, you will never be able to fully complete your purpose on your own.

I've discovered that two separate people are born with two separate purposes in life, yet can actually be born for the same purpose!

> *And as they led him away, they laid hold upon one Simon, a Cyrenian, coming out of the country, and on him they laid the cross, that he might bear it after Jesus. (Lk 23:26,* KJV*)*

For every person pregnant with a purpose, there is a midwife assigned to help them. There is always someone assigned to help you carry the weight or to open the door for you when your hands are full. This is good news because although getting pregnant is natural, it isn't normal. Being pregnant is a natural experience; it's just not normal for you to be in that state. No one spends their entire life pregnant; so it's natural, it's just not normal for them to always be that way. And whatever isn't normal for us will require for someone else to help us navigate through the process. There is no need to remain lost when there is someone nearby who knows the way. There is no need to struggle with a heavy load when there is someone nearby who's capable of helping you lift it and move it. These things happen, but they aren't a normal state. Purpose happens every day, and although it's a natural experience connected to our presence, it isn't a normal state we find ourselves in. We all need help!

Waiting On Help

Waiting for anything isn't easy; let's face it, it's waiting, and that's self-explanatory. But there's something about waiting for help that seems to add an extra layer of frustration, especially when you're pumped and ready to go. Before I go any further, I feel compelled to share with you that waiting patiently, expectantly, and frustratingly all takes the same amount of time. They just don't feel the same or produce the same results! Why did I feel it was necessary to mention that? Because how you decided to wait will determine how *you* will arrive at your destination. Yes, you're going to have to wait, but how you decide to wait will determine if it's just a wait or will it be a "weight" as well.

You're going to need help, and help is coming, so wait for it. Because while you are pregnant with your purpose, someone else is either giving birth or have given birth to theirs. And they just so happen to be the answer to the need you have. Now that you are accepting the idea that you can't get to where you need to go and want to go alone. I figured this would be a good time to slip into the equation that the help you need may not be the help you want.

This Doesn't Look Like What I Was Expecting

Before David became King David, he was only a shepherd boy name David. A young boy whom the prophet Samuel anointed and declared to be the next king in the presence of his father and brothers, because greatness never happens unless there's a witness. See, even greatness itself will need the help of a witness!

The witness will come through the door first, followed by the help. David was in the third trimester of his purpose when his greatness was witnessed then came his help—Goliath. I'm sure this didn't look anything like what he was expecting, hoping, or wanting. It is worth mentioning that Israel didn't have giant problems prior to this. In fact, Goliath didn't show up until after David was anointed to be king. So what are our lessons here? You have not gone far enough into your destiny if you haven't been confronted by a giant. Every king-size anointing will require and attract a giant-size battle in order for you to get into the palace. So get ready for your own Goliath. It will rarely be easy and special at the same time. And your greatness is located in what stands before you that seems impossible. But that's not your impossibility, that's your help. Lastly, you will always be greatly challenged where you are greatly anointed, so accept the fact that greatness is assisted by the challenges it faces.

There's A Battle To Win, So Who Is With Me?

Wisdom is often revealed in the counsel you give, but it will be confirmed by the counsel you seek.

Now that you know you're in the third trimester and that you're going to need help, the natural question is, who is going to help you? Brace yourself; in the third trimester, there are moments of isolation, when God shipwrecks you to a place in your life where your only help comes from Him.

> *I will lift up mine eyes unto the hills, from whence cometh my help.*
> *My help cometh from the LORD, which made heaven and earth. (Ps. 121:1–2, KJV)*

The third trimester isn't like the first, where you have gotten past the morning sickness. It's certainly not like the second trimester, when your glow is evident and purpose looks good on you and you have gotten used to being pregnant. No, this is the third trimester when you're starting to get tired of being pregnant and you just want to give birth already! This is the season you get to know more about your help. This is the season you learn to become totally dependent.

This level of dependency isn't simply the loss of your independence; it's the gain of certainty about your help and your intimacy with your help. No one can truly help you that you can't truly trust. It's not that they can't be trusted, but can "you" trust them? Whenever there isn't complete trust, you will minimize their involvement by constantly restricting their opportunities to help you. Even God can't help you when you limit His opportunities to be your help. Help isn't help until it's allowed to help. So although you are down to the moment that only God can help you, you have to surrender to His help. I must admit this isn't easy to navigate, because it requires you to be the passenger when you want to be the pilot. The passenger feels the turbulence, they feel the bumps, and they have no idea how long this uncomfortable ride will happen or how to get out of it. This is when you must trust the one that got the plane off the ground to also now have the skill to fly it and even land it. This is when you must accept if God was able to place purpose inside you at birth, He can certainly get you to the point of birthing it. As uncomfortable as it may be, sometimes you just have to simply trust what's instore for you. Oftentimes you can't see providence at work until after you have experienced it first.

What's Done In The Dark Is What Comes To Light

I've always believed the most courageous thing anyone can do is to love. Why? Because to send love out doesn't guarantee it will bring love back. Therefore, love is the most courageous thing you can ever do. But running closely tied for second, are trust, intimacy, and dependency. Just like love, each one makes you extremely vulnerable to someone else. Each one says, "You now have the power to hurt me, but I'm placing my confidence in you that you won't." Here's where the separation comes between love and these three. Love can happen out in the open, but trust, intimacy, and dependency can only be confirmed and developed in the dark. In the moments when you are most vulnerable and exposed are the only times their existence can come to light. It's what's done in the dark that often causes things to come to light. What makes light brilliant is often the darkness it pierces through. It's like walking from one lighted room to the next, there is normally no distinction. But have you ever been sound asleep and someone turns the light on? It's that once dark place that reveals the brilliance of the light that now pierces through it. This is how God is in the moments when you feel unsure, insecure and hesitant. This is His moment to shine in your purpose. This moment isn't about you or your baby at all; it's all about the one that will help you deliver it. So watch Him work!

Here Is Where You Find Me

Intimacy is reaching for you in the dark and not just finding you there but discovering you reaching back for me. This gives you the certainty you need that your help cometh.

I will lift up mine eyes unto the hills, from whence cometh my help My help cometh from the Lord, which made heaven and earth. (Ps. 121:1-2)

Believe it or not, you will never become certain about God until there is a season of uncertainty in your life. You won't know for sure if you have an intimate relationship with God until your faith in Him provides Him with an opportunity for His Word to fail you.

> *For he hath said, I will never leave thee, nor forsake thee. (Heb. 13:5, KJV)*

You will never know how much someone is there and will be there for you until there is an opportunity for them not to be. Let's be honest with each other. I'm not going to pretend this is an easy premise to wrap your head around. You're in the third trimester, you're feeling uncomfortable, dependent, and vulnerable. This, by far, is not a great mental and emotional mix. Feeling uncertain and vulnerable can create indecision, and indecision will allow your story to be written by something other than yourself. Circumstance will always snatch the pen out of your hand and take the liberty of writing the rest of your story when you can't decide what you want the rest of your story to look like. Before you hand over your story to your circumstances to finish, keep in mind the hands you're already in make masterpieces out of everything they touch. This is the season when God gets up close and personal and His touch becomes extremely noticeable. Here is where you find Him and His help reveals His proximity.

The Father, The King, And The Master

I found that with God, oftentimes the opposite is true. Sometimes proximity can feel like distance and presence can feel like absence. Oftentimes, the cause of this is because God is not a very effective or active communicator as many would suggest. Not just because God has mastered the art of silence, but because He will switch up His voice in order to teach us how to learn to hear when the Father, the King, or the Master is speaking. God tends to speak in the voice that's consistent with the moment or season He has us in. So there are times when you want to hear from the Father when the King or the Master is speaking. This is only one of the reasons why I said God isn't a very effective communicator.

Another reason is He will reveal the end of the story but hold back details. For instance, He will show Joseph a dream of his forthcoming greatness but hold back the details about the pit, slavery, and prison. I believe that God knows if He shares the details of the journey with us we will never undertake the journey. I also consider God not to be a very effective communicator because He will speak and not tell you when you didn't hear Him. Nor does God revert back to speaking to you as He has in times past, but He will require that your hearing matures to the voice He is now using. He requires you to start hearing on the level that is consistent with the level He is taking you to. Why? Because the level you are hearing will always be consistent with the level of His influence. The more influence God has with you, the greater the impact He can make through you. He wants you to not only hear on that level for impact but also establish intimacy. Real intimacy is manifested when you are able to hear the whisper of the one you are intimate with speaking above the shouts of everything else. He whispers in moments of struggles, stress, and strain because He knows a whisper can only be heard when you either lean in to hear or allow someone to have access to your ear. This whisper in the dark is when you reach for Him and not only find Him but also discover He is also reaching back for you. These are the moments that you learn personally what it means when He said, "Lo, I am with you always!"

In the third trimester, you learn all that you need to know about your help because it's the moment when your help isn't just helpful, it's intimate.

Awkward But Secure

Discipline is the cornerstone for any level of sustainability. Nothing disciplines your trust more than the third trimester. A discipline that sustains you is a discipline you have developed in your moments in the dark.

You may feel awkward, but this is the season of your life that has proven most of all that you are secure. Because it has developed your discipline, and rarely do we lose what discipline has built. It's also the season that has developed your stamina, and that's just what you need to give birth and to fulfill your purpose. Your stamina is a revelation of your convictions, because your press reveals how convinced you are that "it's" going to happen. No, you're not as graceful as you were when you first started this journey, and yes, you have picked up some weight (critics and naysayers along the way), but you're confident that this is going to happen. You're now able to say, "He got me, and I'm confident I can do this." That's the perfect mind-set to have in the third trimester. The only time criticism and doubt become stronger than purpose is when you allow them to become greater than your own opinion of yourself.

This is the third trimester; you're in the home stretch! This is when you defiantly say, "I'm not going to grant anyone the opportunity to make a contribution to my failure who hasn't made any contribution to my success."

Graceful and *victorious* don't have to always share the same space. Therefore, there are moments when providence is guiding your steps that you will actually stumble into the winner's circle. So accept the fact the dream won't always have dreamy moments. Besides, victory and success will always look good on the résumé of greatness. And no one will know how the battle went, just who won.

> And when Gideon was come, behold, there was a man that told a dream unto his fellow, and said, Behold, I dreamed a dream, and, lo, a cake of barley bread tumbled into the host of Midian, and came unto a tent, and smote it that it fell, and overturned it, that the tent lay along.
>
> And his fellow answered and said, This is nothing else save the sword of Gideon the son of Joash, a man of Israel: for into his hand hath God delivered Midian, and all the host. (Judg. 7:13–14, KJV)

You were born to do this! You've carried this all your life, and now you will carry it across the finish line. Even if you have to stumble across, you're going over. So if greatness and purpose have rewarded you with their trust, reward them with your faith in their election of you. This is the third trimester, and your help is with you.

Everything and everyone is falling into position. Don't ignore this, this is God's hand! This is your help helping. The third trimester will produce relationships and opportunities, neither of which just happens. They will always involve or need something else in order to form their existence. There isn't a chance meeting or opportunity because your purpose and destiny is too great for God to leave them to happenstance. Providence grabs hold of people, places, situations, time, and you in its hand and mixes you together for the success of your purpose. The distance you have traveled has merited what is coming to help you across the finish line. I'm very excited for you because it won't be long now!

8

Labor Pains

IT'S GO TIME! A contraction—the unrelenting will of your purpose pushing on your ability to birth it. This is the moment that you finally realize that purpose is a reality, that it's more uncomfortable not to do something than to do it. It's also the moment when you realize your choices have been stripped. This is going to happen; greatness is a nearing reality. The instant that both trepidation and excitement share the same space in your mind, you're having labor pains.

You're excited and nervous because you know what comes after this: more pain, more discomfort, and more pushing. But also the birthing of what you've been waiting for, hoping for, and preparing for! Doubt and joy fill your mind with things that experience has yet to reveal. This is the moment you realize that oftentimes, the difference between being extraordinary and mediocre is being an ounce more dedicated to your dream than being afraid to do it.

The moment when it becomes uncomfortable to carry your gift and dream any further, that's confirmation you have the ability to give birth to it. When you have a sense that there isn't any more preparation you can make for its arrival, that's when it's time to embrace its arrival. When the *who, how, what,* and *where* have all been answered and you're now left with *when,* it's time. Every dream or vision has to answer each of those questions, and the *when* is the most difficult of them to answer because it requires your patience and not your ability. It's also the most exciting question because that means there is a birth date! You have to learn to set a due date to give birth because without it, you put no pressure on your dream to get here, and you take the pressure off yourself to bring it here. I know the Bible tells us, "Do not be anxious about anything," (Phil. 4:6, NIV), but it never said not to be excited. Due dates are a part of vision, and people who don't have a vision (or a due date) don't have anything to get excited about or to look forward to. Your internal pressure to birth is your labor pain. It's all part of a natural progression.

It's Go Time!

Pain is a symptom, not a condition.

Pain happens for various reasons, from something being infected, to something being out of order, to experiencing resistance, to experiencing the introduction of life. Yes, that's what I said; pain is an introduction of life. Life is never brought forth in the absence of struggle or discomfort. Perhaps it's because whatever is brought forth in struggle is cherished. And that explains the reason why people who fight to get something will put up a fight to keep it. I always understood the real value of anything has less to do with the price of it and more to do with the cost of it. The real value of anything you have or own is in what it cost *you*! What you gave up to get it, what you sacrificed, or what you endured for it—that's where the reveal value lies. I always believed God over paid for our salvation because the price of salvation was a man, but the cost of it was Jesus, God in the form of a man.

For what the law could not do, in that it was weak through the flesh, God sending his own Son in the likeness of sinful flesh, and for sin, condemned sin in the flesh: (Rom. 8:3, KJV)

Whatever the cause or the reason for pain, no doubt when it happens, it will always require and demand attention. The internal pressure and excitement you're experiencing is your purpose demanding your complete focus. Purpose presses you with deadlines, requests, and events that bring you into the center of where you're supposed to be at that exact moment. It's go time! The internal pressure and excitement to give birth is destiny's and purpose's way of telling you tomorrow is no longer tomorrow, it's today.

And we know that all things work together for good to them that love God, to them who are the called according to his purpose. (Rom. 8:28, KJV)

Pain zeros in your focus. When purpose is ready to launch you, oftentimes, the pain it produces is pressure. Pressure is an advocate of those who dare to live an extraordinary life! How so? Besides pressure-producing and confirming greatness, it alleviates the power of distractions. Those under pressure typically have one goal; to deal with whatever is bringing the pressure. When you're under pressure, your habits change, especially your mental habits. That's why labor pains before birthing are a major benefit because your mental habits will become your actual realities; what you constantly think, you will consistently do.

For as he thinketh in his heart, so is he. (Prov. 23:7, kjv)

Labor pains before birthing is a gift that the process of purpose provides you. The pressure from a sudden shift will always awaken your focus and concentration. This simply means you no longer have the choice to be lackadaisical or unfocused; it's go time! And those who don't know what time it is will never know when it's time to move. You can never be successful at anything when your timing is off. Timing is the harmony of life; it keeps efforts in line with the goal they serve.

Believe it or not, the pressure you are under is your baby returning a favor to you for carrying it all this time. It's your purpose making you aware you've begun the countdown to greatness. The old saying is "No pain, no gain." In this instance, I couldn't agree more. All the multiple activities, demands, and pressures on you now have just notified you that you're at the forefront of the receiving end of purpose. So now is the time. Do whatever it takes to move into position to birth because you will never get what you're not in position to receive. Getting it to position is a revelation of what you are expecting for yourself. And that satisfies the law of attraction, which says you can never attract anything for your benefit that you don't expect. When you don't expect it, you don't make room or provision for it. Your labor-pain moment is wisdom speaking through experience. It will always be neglectful and certainly foolish to waste any amount of wisdom that a moment is providing. The season of discomfort is purpose teaching you the lesson of position and readiness.

Don't waste the moment, season, or reason for this pressure and excitement just focusing on the cause of it. Use this moment to raise the level of your thoughts and awareness because the pressure you're currently under and the excitement you're feeling came to bring about a major shift in your thinking. Every shift in your life ought to produce a shift in your thinking. Therefore, no one has minor thoughts just before a major experience. I'm sure you will attest to the fact that there's no partnership without agreement. This moment you're in should find a partner in the thoughts you are thinking because what is birthed in harmony enters in precisely where it is expected!

We're Taking On Water

Choice is a grace. It's wonderful to be able to make up your own mind; that's why choice is a grace because it allows you to retain ownership of your life. When you give up your choices, you surrender ownership of your life—well, at least in the area that you no longer have choices. That's what happens when the water breaks; purpose has just taken away your choices and your ownership of your life. Deals have been made, contracts have been signed, you have put your signature on lease agreements or have even taken purchase orders, your water has broken.

Let me see if I can explain in this manner. Imagine being a captain of a ship who has chartered a course toward a new exploration when suddenly, you're experiencing rough waters and you decide it's best to turn back. The only problem is you can't see what you left behind anymore. And your compass only points north; straight ahead is your only option.

That's how purpose works for those who are focused on being all they were created to be. Purpose will cause you to lose sight of your past; you remember what it was like, but you can't see it being your life anymore. You lost your choices, and your life is now in the hands of the course you are taking; it's in the hands of purpose.

Nothing like the reality of your dream will produce your drive for greatness. Reality can't be denied—it can be misinterpreted, but it certainly can't be denied. Labor pains and water breaking are moments that can't be denied. Misinterpreted, yes, because no one can tell you for sure if it will be an hour from now or twenty hours from now, but one thing is certain: it's coming. It's the moments of sudden shifts in your life and reality that communicate the certainty that your purpose is coming. It can be before the due date or somewhat afterward; one thing for sure, it's coming. You can feel it, you know it. It's the power of knowing that will fuel your drive for greatness and that should ignite your tenacity to the point that you refuse to yield to contentment or mediocrity.

Your water breaking, the sudden shifts in your reality—these come to reveal there is an outstanding expectation and anticipation about to be fulfilled. This is go time. Isn't that exciting?

Are Your Bags Packed?

No one will intentionally move into a benefit they haven't prepared for.

Rarely does opportunity give advance notice, but labor pains are your advance notice. The sudden shift in your reality and sudden surge of excitement aren't just noticeable, they're directional. They're steering you and pulling everything else in your life in the direction of your purpose. Your purpose and dream are like gravity. If the entire world suddenly tilted, even gravity would agree with it and begin to pull everything in the direction the world is slanted. However, there will be some that will defiantly resist going in the direction that greatness and purpose is forcing their life in and is steering them toward. When your labor pains begin and your bags aren't packed, you're not prepared to move in the direction of your greatness; you're just content to know which direction it is pointing you in. Start moving toward the direction you're being pulled in, called to, purposed for. That's the only way to give birth and to satisfy your internal appetite to be great.

Don't let all your critical thinking be done by your critics. The sudden shift in your reality is assessment time. This is the time for you to find fault. Why? Because you can never improve on what you don't see as a problem. There are some things that you have to improve on in order to keep pace with your destiny. Because destiny doesn't wait for you; but it will force you to catch up to it. You don't want the reason that you have to play catch up is because your bags should have been packed and weren't. Remember, I mentioned earlier the importance of timing: "You can never be successful at anything when you're timing is off" and "Timing is the harmony of life; it keeps efforts in line with the goal they serve."

Everything worthwhile is worth a second look. Pain and pressure are always moments for reexamination and reassessment. Whatever you look at twice, you get to learn about it twice. It gives you an opportunity to determine, "Do I have everything I need for this moment, is everything and everyone in place? Are we moving at the correct pace or in the right direction?" Whenever there is a learning opportunity, there is a growth moment. However, we don't always get to choose our opportunities for growth. Sometimes, the moment is chosen for us. The moments of labor pains are simply your purpose choosing a moment for you to grow into position.

Whenever God intends to inspire or ignite the growth of something, He stretches it. Your labor pains are the final growth spurt before delivery. This happens because God never intends for the process to kill the one it was intended to bless, so He grows you through the process that will also bring you into your greatness. You need to understand you're like gold: gold is never melted down to be destroyed but reframed for another purpose. This is not your destruction but preparation. Pressure always prepares the destined for their destiny.

> *But as for you, ye thought evil against me; but God meant it unto good, to bring to pass, as it is this day, to save much people alive. (Gen. 50:20,* kjv*)*

The pressure you are under is because God knows if given a choice, most people—even those of us who would be great—will stop growing. People who stop growing and progressing live in unproductive cycles. The only way to break a cycle is to make a change, so pressure is a change breaking a cycle because it creates different behavior patterns. The sudden shift in your life circumstances is oftentimes the change that's mandated to outgrow an infertile cycle.

You can't go into a productive season dressed in a sterile mind-set; the experience of labor pains redresses your kingdom mind-set. The advent of growth and change are adversity and pain, but they are also the geneses of restoration.

> *And he said, A certain man had two sons:*
> *And the younger of them said to his father, Father, give me the portion of goods that falleth to me. And he divided unto them his living.*
> *And not many days after the younger son gathered all together, and took his journey into a far country, and there wasted his substance with riotous living.*

And when he had spent all, there arose a mighty famine in that land; and he began to be in want.

And he went and joined himself to a citizen of that country; and he sent him into his fields to feed swine.

And he would fain have filled his belly with the husks that the swine did eat: and no man gave unto him.

And when he came to himself, he said, How many hired servants of my father's have bread enough and to spare, and I perish with hunger!

I will arise and go to my father, and will say unto him, Father, I have sinned against heaven, and before thee (Lk 15:11–18, KJV)

God uses labor pains to restore, reset, or expand your kingdom mind-set. Why? A kingdom mind-set is how you are able to recognize the limitations of the level you're currently on. You can't produce or birth your next thinking on a low level. A kingdom mind-set will help you to understand that the level you are on or the environment you are in can no longer present you with new challenges and, therefore, can no longer provide you with opportunities. He restores your kingdom mind-set so you won't reach backward while moving forward because whenever your mind is divided, so will be your efforts.

The season of labor pains are the continuations of your growth, and people who continue to grow and progress are always in pursuit of something. I once heard this line spoken by Burt Reynolds in an old black-and-white cowboy show, and not only did it stick with me, but also I thought it was so befitting to anyone in pursuit of their purpose in life: "The fruit you must reach for is better than that which falls to your feet." What you gain from your pursuit is always going to be much better than what you stumble upon on the side of the road. The growth that is intentional will always yield better fruit than that which was circumstantial.

A Few More Items To Add To Your Suitcase

God can't add to our growth without teaching us something new. With all our preparations and growth, some lessons can only be taught and learned at the same time.

The season of labor pains teaches us new lessons that we can only learn in those moments. Below are a few; others, I'm sure you will discover some additional ones on your own as they relate to your individual purpose and experiences. And as you do, make sure you add them to your bags.

New Lessons:

_____

_____

_____

The closer you get to the fulfilling your purpose, the more you come to the realization how many people are now standing on the sideline. One of the greatest pains in life comes from feeling isolated and being isolated. Being alone will make your dream suddenly feel like a nightmare. Labor pains happen because there are some moments and even distances you can only cover alone. Why? Because nothing reveals or confirms the level of your commitment to anything until you have to do it by yourself. Two factors of being or feeling alone are the following: First, if you have to always look around to see who is going with you, you're less likely to go. Next, if you're waiting for the perfect conditions to get started, you will have the perfect excuse never to try. Pack with you your willingness to go because those who will fulfill their purpose must be willing to do what others won't even consider doing.

New Lessons:

_____

_____

_____

_____

_____

Why is purpose first a dream before it becomes a reality? A dream is how God gives you a glimpse of your future without giving you an opportunity to doubt it. Dreams are the only place your faith can go that your doubts can't follow. Have you ever noticed we believe everything in our dreams, to the point that oftentimes, we even awaken from them with real-life responses? Purpose had to begin as a dream in order to gain the cooperation of you confidence.

When you're not confident in yourself, you won't be confident about your future, and you will never move into a future that you're not confident about. Pack into your bags your confidence. Why? Because confidence translates into ability. Also, you will never step voluntarily into a future you don't see yourself in.

New Lessons:

_____

_____

_____

_____

_____

Packing actually requires thinking. People who are not thinking, dreaming, or envisioning their next destination are not going to get there. Why? Because you will only cover the distance you are willing to envision. Your growth and potential are oftentimes consistent with the level of your curiosity, thoughts, dreams, and visions. Pack into your bags your curiosity. Why? Because attention and activity will always go where interest already exists. Attention and activity are natural responses to interest. It's impossible to be absent and inattentive in the places that hold your attention and interest.

New Lessons:

_____

_____

_____

_____

_____

Your growth, maturity, and potential won't just come from how you react to experiences but also how you respond after the experiences are over.

Who and what you will ultimately become will be determined by how you respond to everything that has happened to you and everything you've been through. How you respond to something will determine what happens in your life from that point forward and how it will impact your life from that point forward. Pack into your bags your ability to respond and not react. Why? Because when you respond, you maintain your power. When you react, you give it away.

This Is The Reason For The Season

Pregnancy and purpose will never happen out of order. No doubt that the primary purpose of being pregnant is to give birth, but I believe it also serves as an example for the necessity of having and establishing order. And no season more than the season of labor pains reveals the necessity and the existence of order. Labor pains bring anticipation as well as awareness of what's the next step. Sudden shifts in your current reality reveal that your next step is a new reality.

Because God is a cyclical God, He moves in cycles and seasons. Seasons not only reveal natural order, but also provide opportunities for preparation while creating the expectation in this season of what has been promised to you by the previous season.

As uncomfortable as this season is, it's necessary because it reveals that things are happening in order. God cannot be a God of divine design and not be a God of divine order. And so purpose is subjected to the natural order of destiny; that includes labor pains. This season means you have ascended onto the stage of graduation and are sitting through the procession, the speeches, and acknowledgements; just for the moment to turn the tassel!

> *For God is not a God of disorder but of peace. (1 Cor. 14:33,* NIV*)*

When God wants to bring us into a new season of destiny or purpose, He may shift the paradigm of things, but He will never shift the order of them. He simply creates out of the order He has already established.

God establishes order to manifest His will; like His Word, order brings the will of God into the visual range of His people.

This is not the season to pivot directions; this is the season to embrace the moment and what it comes to do. The season of labor pains comes to confirm that order is what connects now to next. This is the final hurdle, the linchpin to birth. Yes, it's uncomfortable, but it will always be uncomfortable when your current chapter is starting to be intruded upon by your next chapter. This is what happens when there's a crowning of tomorrow.

Don't Break The Order Of Things

Order is a nonnegotiable: don't touch it, let it run its course! "Don't touch it, let it run its course"—have you ever heard those words? Normally, what's behind them is much wisdom. When something gets out of order, it potentially becomes vulnerable. Order will determine what a season, a moment, an environment, and even an individual will produce. Barrenness is not always a lack of ability; sometimes it's a lack of order. A person out of order becomes the barren ground in their own life. A barren ground produces nothing but frustration and disappointment. The lack of order will produce a lack of preparation, and you will wait forever for something you haven't conditioned your life for. I've found you will always spend more time waiting for something than you do preparing for it, because when there is no preparation for it there will be no realization of it.

It's labor pains, yes, but it's birthing's introduction.

Closing Chapter

There is never a new chapter without an old one closing. Chapters are the experiences and lessons that form the books we call our life and purpose. There are many ends, because there are many brand new beginnings. You have traveled well and grown much through your chapters. Although you have yet to give birth, this is worth mentioning, because you can't simply measure a person by their destination, but by the distance they have traveled. You have come far, through many frustration, uncertainties and challenges. Your labor pain season is the end of your season of pregnancy and the beginning of your birthing. Are you ready to give birth? I hope you are ready, because coming this far you have certainly earned the opportunity!

9

Giving Birth

THE BIRTHING OF anything worthwhile will not only take perseverance but also cause fatigue.

Every mother is most exhausted before the last push, suggesting that whatever has owned you up to this point will demand that you push beyond the temptations to quit and rest in order for you to possess it. In the greatest moments of your life, your insistence must always be present because some things can only be claimed by your last ounce of strength.

The Bible lets us know that Joshua and the children of Israel walked around the walls of Jericho once each day for six days, but on the seventh day, they walked seven times and still had the strength to shout the walls down. And not only shout, but also they found the strength to run in and take the city once the walls had fallen. Where did they find the strength to fight and take it after walking around the entire city seven times on the seventh day? It may have everything to do with what the *Smith's Bible Dictionary* interprets the name Jericho to mean. According to *Smith's Bible Dictionary*, the name Jericho means "Place of Fragrance." Now I completely understand where the strength came from because when your dream and purpose is so close that the sweet aroma of it reveals the proximity of it, how could you not push into it? So this is the moment and season you decide that every ounce of strength is a worthwhile exchange for the chance to hold your dream in the bosom of your life.

Whatever it is—a dream, vision, business, or purpose—when it's time to give birth to it, it is the moment you find in you what you didn't know you already possessed. A resolve and strength to give birth and be great can only be revealed by the exhaustion of the moment. The moment to give birth is when the pursuit of anything worthwhile forces a decision upon you; it forces you to decide to either listen to your fatigue or the sweet fragrance of your goal revealing to you it is close.

The Dilemma

Often, greater than pain is fatigue.

Fatigue is such a monstrous battle to win that many will surrender their dream to their struggle. Not because it's hard but because it's exhausting. It was Shakespeare who wrote, "Fatigue makes cowards of us all." It's often hard to find the courage to push, to take another step, to lunge forward one more time when everything you're feeling, thinking, and experiencing suggests you won't survive the next energy extraction. Fatigue is the killer of faith and dreams. It's a dilemma because you have been pregnant for so long and you've endured so many changes, pains, and hurdles, and now you're at the finish line, crossing it feels like it will finish you! You want it, but you're apprehensive. Apprehension allows the promise of difficulty to create patterns of frustration and failure in your life. "I want it, but I'm exhausted, what do I do?" You must push on! Apprehension is one of those things your feelings will purchase for you that you cannot afford. Fear, fatigue, and apprehension will cause you to go over your emotional budget. Believe it or not, although you can't afford to be fatigued, you can afford to be tired.

You Have To Learn To Be Tired

If you want to be great, if you want to fulfill your purpose, if you want to give birth, you're going to have to be tired. In order to move into your greatness, you have to learn to be more tired than you are fatigued. You're going to have to be more tired of being ordinary and unfulfilled than you are fatigued by the pursuit of greatness. This is the reason why you can afford being tired but not fatigued, especially since becoming fatigued while in transition to your dream and then succumbing to it is indication you have resolved that here is where you belong. So until you get tired of where you are, you will never get to where you divinely belong or where you always hoped to be. Being fatigued while in pursuit of your dream is actually making a decision to run from it. So I must advise you that it takes more energy to run from something than it does to run to something. Running from your moment just because it's hard will have a more emotional and mental drain on your strength than it will take to accomplish it. The energy you won't use in pursuit of your purpose and dreams will be bested by the energy it will take to reconcile the rest of your life with your regrets. Yes, giving birth is difficult, but difficult isn't the same as impossible!

Desire Is Never Fatigued, But It Is Tired

You get to decide if you will possess what you already own.

The pursuit of anything worthwhile will have a moment of fatigue that will not only reveal how bad you want it but also decide if you get it.

When you're fatigued, it's easy to put your dream down with the promise to pick it up later. Bad move! Procrastination is the single biggest threat to what's next and what's possible now. Procrastination often arises out of insecurity, doubt, and fear, and if these feelings are not dealt with, they will become the root cause of procrastination in the future. Even if you can't remember why you put something off, you can't forget the feelings that are connected to why you did it. Your feelings will always be hardwired to the dream and the decisions surrounding it. The effects of procrastination mostly show up in missed opportunities. Even opportunities that may show up later will potentially suffer from your procrastination now because when it's easy to say you're too tired now, it will be easy to say it's too late later.

Your desire to be great has to be greater than your reality and struggle so that you can continue to move forward even when your circumstances and fatigue are telling you that you have reached your end. Your thirst must always exceed your reach. That's how progress continues, because thirst is a desire that pulls you forward. I always believed no one can ignore their own thirst. That's good because thirst is a passion that can't subside or be satisfied on its own; it must be dealt with. As relentless as the thirst, so is the behavior that it causes. That's why desire is never fatigued, although it's tired. Desire is a thirst that's tired of being thirsty. Desire is a thirst that's tired of being ordinary. Desire is a thirst that's tired of not living the life it's meant to live.

If your dreams have not at least reached the level of your need to push, then I must resolve, though it's possible, that you're very fatigued, but you're not tired enough. It's possible to carry something for a long time but not carry it very far. Being tired will cause you to carry the dream across the finish line. If I was preaching in my church right now, I would poll the congregation and ask how many people are tired of living beneath their divine purpose, tired of not seeing their dream overtake their life. And for those who acknowledge that they are tired, my answer would have been, "Then push." So my response to you is push!

You must learn to be tired but not fatigued. Why? Because whenever God wants to reveal greatness in you or through you, He will give you something to obey. And when He wants to bless you with something great, He gives you something to pursue. Now do you have an unwavering desire to pursue and to push, knowing your greatness and blessing is on the other side of your last push?

I heard talk show host, radio personality, and game show host Steve Harvey recall his experience with working out with famed bodybuilder Lee Haney. According to Steve, Lee will often urge him to give him one more rep. Steve indicated that not only did he do it, but it was Steve's mind-set for doing it that got my attention.

Steve said, "I can always give you one more, if that's all you're asking. I can give you one more of whatever it is!" This is it, that's what extraordinary is: it's adding extra to ordinary. Can you push one more time beyond the fatigue and difficulty you may presently be facing? It will be the single most important thing you do from going from who you were to who you're created to be.

Anything But Pushing Is Unacceptable

What you learn to tolerate you must learn to live with because whatever you learn to tolerate, you give it permission to become your norm.

Anything but giving birth can't be tolerated because once you tolerate not giving birth, you give permission to being unfruitful to become your norm. But who are we kidding here? It's time to give birth. You know it, I know it, and so does everything else that doesn't want you to do it. I guess it's worth mentioning at this point that everything and everyone hanging around will not be excited about what's about to take place in your life.

You need to understand that those whom you have allowed in your orbit who cannot get excited about your accomplishments are secretly competing against you. And they are also competing for your dream, but not for the same reasons you're competing for it. You're competing to move your life forward and to realize your dream and to fulfill your purpose. They are competing for it so they can keep their place, influence, and presence in your life. Oftentimes, when you are birthing your dream, you will find that people you love will become people who are hard to live with, associate with, or to be around. Some will even launch accusations at you that you've changed. And let's hope they are right; when you're pregnant, you are supposed to change.

Once an authentic dream becomes a genuine goal, there will always be measureable and noticeable change in the dreamer. The direction you're looking in and moving in reveals where your mind lives, but the change that you make reveals where it has moved to. I always believed your internal journey hasn't covered much territory if you haven't changed and if your perspective hasn't changed since you've begun your pursuit. You and your perspective are supposed to reflect your goal through your actions, choices, and attitude. Everything about you is supposed to look like the direction you are looking in and heading in.

Every drastic change in behavior follows a drastic change in thinking. You're acting like someone giving birth because you're thinking like someone giving birth. Don't you change that mind-set; in fact, remember this: both the expectant mother and birthing mother's mind-set never conforms to those around her; everyone around her changes their mind-set to hers. From her household, to her extended family, to the doctors, the nurses, and the hospital staff, they all conform. What's the point? Keep moving; eventually everything around you will conform, even the wall that's in the way! It will eventually move or fall down!

When you move into the birthing seasons of your life, there will always be distractions. Why? Because the enemy always fights the hardest just before you break through and into promise.

Now Jericho was straitly shut up because of the children of Israel: none went out, and none came in. (Josh. 6:1, KJV)

Distractions are an indication you're at the end of the struggle and at the beginning of the reward. So don't get distracted—not here, not now. Because if your attention and strength is divided, so will be the results they produce. The best way to kill the potential of something is to take away what it needs. If desire is divided from strength and focus, it can't produce on the same level as it could with them. This is where you need to recognize that fatigue is often an indication it's time to make a change, that something in your life is contrary to your strength and effectiveness. You can't have a divided focus and it not produce a divided agenda. And you can't have a divided agenda and have complete success. Because whenever your focus and agendas are divided, so will be your loyalties. When your loyalties are divided, your strength is divided. You can't birth your purpose or dream out of your weakness; you need your strength. Contrary to what you may believe, being fatigued isn't weakness—it's an indication your strength is being used to its full capacity; it's an indication that you are in the midst of birthing!

There comes a moment during the birthing that regardless how exhausted the mother is, all she wants to do is push. In fact, there are times when the doctor may have to slow her down and reset her pace. Her desire to push when she is completely exhausted says her second wind is coming from both her determination and anticipation. It's a revelation that at this point, anything other than pushing is unacceptable. There's something about the human nature that the arrival of adversity and struggle oftentimes produces the opposite response than what was originally intended by the struggle. It produces a tenacious spirit to succeed and to overcome. If you keep pushing and moving forward, you will discover that the problem, struggle, and fatigue somehow releases your resolve;

you won't accept anything less than birthing your dream. That's major because what you accept sets the precedence for everything that will follow. It's only through the pushing that you will reap rewards beyond what were your original intentions and hope.

> *Now unto him that is able to do exceeding abundantly above all that we ask or think, according to the power that worketh in us (Eph. 3:20, KJV)*

Lying Down But Not Lying Still

Birthing and pushing are never separated.

I've come to realize that nothing happens until something moves. Movement is like a magnet; it draws your will, desires, and efforts in the direction of your goal. Movement reconciles the contradiction between what you know and what you see. Movement gives the yes in your spirit veto power over the no in your sight. Especially since a yes isn't a yes unless there is a supporting succeeding action. Every decision must have the backing of an action; if not, it's only a thought!

> *When she had heard of Jesus, came in the press behind, and touched his garment.*
> *And Jesus, immediately knowing in himself that virtue had gone out of him, turned him about in the press, and said, Who touched my clothes? (Mk 5:30, KJV)*

Every dimension of glory, purpose, and greatness is accessed through movement; whether the matrix is obedience, faith, or pushing, there must be movement. So this is certainly not the time to be still, so if you think you're supposed to do nothing, your dream will produce nothing. Also take note, giving birth to your dream differs from natural birth. Just because it's time to do it doesn't mean it's just going to happen for you; greatness is decided, and it's decided by your activity. So yes, this is the right time, but time is only the opportunity for what is supposed to happen, not the cause of it. So when it's time to give birth, it's time to give yourself to it; in doing so, you have to make time for it. Giving your all to your goals is how you argue against your circumstances and obstacles that you deserve what you're pursuing.

When you're pushing, you're signifying that you understand that regardless how much you want something, doesn't mean you deserve it. But it also is an indication that no matter how much it's being withheld from you, it won't be denied to you. Your pushing means you have all the time it takes to make your dream your reality. That's major for any level of success because you don't deserve what you don't make time for, and whatever you don't have time for, you can best believe you don't have room for it as well. Time is how you make space for something to become a part of your life.

Every mother falls deeper in love with the baby who's in her arms than the one who was previously in her womb. She didn't know she could love her baby more until she held what she pushed out. What's my point? If you never allow yourself to be inconvenienced, you will never learn what your efforts have secretly promised to you. And when you push, you will always get more from your purpose and dreams than you give to them.

In 2008, Cadillac had a brilliant ad that said, "When you turn your car on, does it return the favor?" They were suggesting that the simple *pushing* of a button will yield so much more than the effort it took to push it. Now that you know that pursuing your dream and purpose will do more for you than you can do for it, I'm sure you agree that anything other than pushing is unacceptable.

Keep Your Eye On The Prize

It doesn't have to become invisible to disappear.

I remember traveling home from a conference that I taught at and was immediately reminded of the necessity of keeping my eye on the prize. My wife was in the passenger seat because regardless of how tired I am, she usually makes me drive—or should I say, she insists that I always have the privilege of being her chauffer.

Because I was very familiar with the way home, I went into autopilot, and there was my mistake. As we were nearing our exit, I got distracted in my conversation with my wife about the slow driver ahead of us, the power of the conference, and the fellowship we had afterwards, and as a result, we ended up missing our exit. My mind was too consumed with where I've been, what I had experienced, and what was currently going on that I lost sight of where I was going.

Because I didn't navigate my moment and opportunity properly, I was now being forced to travel farther down the expressway to the next exit. And this is when I immediately noticed four things about distractions. The first was when you're getting close to your goal, the last thing you need or want to do is to take your eyes off it because it won't become invisible, but it will disappear.

Next, I realized that people who lose their focus can potentially cause their goals to become a casualty to their methods. Granted, this wasn't the case here, but it certainly can be the case concerning your dreams. Afterward, I realized being distracted at a critical moment will drag others into the consequences of my distractions. Although my wife sat there patiently, she had to endure the consequences that my negligence created.

Lastly, I realized it's going to take me much longer now to get back on course than it did for me to get off course. I once read about something called interruption science, which states we can easily get distracted every fifteen minutes and it can take twice as long to get back on course. If it takes you longer to get back on course, it will take you twice as long to reach your destination and give birth to your dream. As you are now in a position to give birth to your goal, don't lose sight of it, and don't go on autopilot. Due diligence is the insurance that the dreamer places on their dream.

Pushing Is A Response And An Understanding

You determine your capacity by your response.

You determine the capacity of your next by your response to your now. What you are set to give birth to now sets the stage for what you will have the ability to give birth to later. Now I'm not promising you that the next birth will be easier—after all, it's birth—but experience does make the process manageable.

Pushing is your response and your understanding of this moment. When you have gotten to the moment of giving birth, there's nothing left to do but push to birth it. Your only response is the most necessary one. Although it's your only response, it's not just what you do but also how you do it that matters. So make sure you respond to this moment with all the positivity and joy it deserves because you have been chosen for this amazing experience! You were born pregnant to give birth to your purpose and dream, so appreciate it regardless of what it demands of you and from you. Besides, gratitude attracts generosity; the moments you're grateful for now attract those you will have an opportunity to be grateful for later.

Lastly, the greatest changes and accomplishments you will experience in your lifetime are the ones you participate in. Your response is your participation in your dream. How you respond to the greatest moments in your life is a major part of your participation in those moments.

So aren't you grateful you were born pregnant? Because now you can participate in the birthing of something that, besides your own children, will be the greatest accomplishment of your life.

Holding The Baby

There are those rare moments when your imagination pales in comparison to your reality.

Inspiration and strength enter your life from many avenues; this is the reason why none of us can afford to close off all the roads. What you will oftentimes need doesn't come dressed in the manner you expected.

For instance, I was sitting in the dentist's office many years ago; it's a place, like many of you, I dread going to. It also was the last place I expected to get any inspiration. I noticed a poster on the wall that got my attention. I initially thought I saw it because I was nervous and was trying to divert my nervous energy elsewhere. Soon after, however, I tried to give myself credit for seeing it because I'm somewhat of an intellectual scavenger; I like picking up ideas, principles, or concepts from the environment or moment I'm in. But the truth is, inspiration and strength enter your life in ways least expected so they can have the full impact that they were intended to have.

The poster in the dental clinic read, "Every great accomplishment was once considered an impossible task" (author unknown).

Accomplishment is the source of renewed strength. Accomplishment is when the outcome will give explanation to the journey. As when a mother holds her baby for the first time that her excitement and strength returns to her, what once fatigued her now restores her. What she gave life to is now bringing life back into her. As she nourishes her baby, it feeds her soul. Yes, this is love, but this is also appreciation for the presence of what she gave birth to because now she suddenly knows as much as her baby needed her to give birth to it, she herself needed to give birth to the baby.

As much as your purpose needs you to finish the course, you will undoubtedly discover you needed you to finish as well. Once a mother births her child, she is forever a mother. Who you are destined to be is in what you give birth to, and once you do it, you will forever be what you were purposed to be. Nothing reverses history, and it will always live from the moment it happens. Nothing will ever reverse the history you're about to make, and it will forever live in the annals of greatness.

Storyteller

No part of this journey can be considered an accident or a coincidence. You would probably think that it was planned from the beginning, and it was, but even more, it was arranged before there was a beginning. You were picked ahead of the creation of time itself to be a story that God wanted to tell about Himself. A story about how He has the unique ability to take ordinary people and impregnate them to do extraordinary work.

> The Word became flesh and made his dwelling among us.
> (Jn 1:14, NIV)

From the moment God spoke, "Let there be light," the order and patterns of God was to always make His Word flesh. To make it a tangible reality in the life of His people. Including the Word He spoke over your life. He wanted your purpose to dwell amongst "us," (us being the entire world). Thanks for saying yes so we can have what He was only able to bring forth through you.

Congratulations, Hand Out The Cigars

What you don't learn to appreciate you will automatically learn to take for granted.

The moment you start to take anything for granted is the moment you start to lose it. You can't protect the presence, health, or welfare of anything you haven't learned to appreciate. Learn to enjoy and to celebrate your accomplishment because your attitude is the first thing that you will impregnate your baby with. Attitude and culture are synonymous; an environment that's positive is already successful at something.

Now that you have given birth, it's time to raise it. I can't wait to see the mark you leave on the world!